Altar

"With my crazy schedule, very few books are able to capture my attention so thoroughly that I neglect my own writing for days. Kimberley's story is not only compelling; it is also important for each of us who needs to be reminded that God is there in our toughest seasons—and will walk us through them, hand in hand, if we only will let Him. I loved this book, and I know you will too."

—SHAUNTI FELDHAHN
Best-selling author, *For Women Only*

"Guys aren't supposed to read books that are written for women, right? Well, I read this one, and it opened my eyes to the pain of rejection. *Left at the Altar* is a must-read for guys too! Besides the fact that it is well written and keeps you wanting to read more, it also works on your soul in the areas of sensitivity and understanding—two traits most of us guys could really use a ton of help with."

—DAVE GUDGEL
Author, *Before You Get Engaged*
and *Before You Live Together*

This is not just a book; it is a love letter of hope—the ultimate reference for any woman facing rejection. Inside you learn not only how to manage rejection but also that God's plan and intention for your life is much better than what you could ever imagine. It has been a lifeline for me . . . one I now offer to you. Reading it you realize God did not waste Kimberley's heartache and tears.

—SHARON
Bel Air, MD

Left at the Altar

*My Story of Hope and Healing for Every Woman
Who Has Felt the Heartbreak of Rejection*

Kimberley Kennedy

THOMAS NELSON
Since 1798

NASHVILLE   DALLAS   MEXICO CITY   RIO DE JANEIRO   BEIJING

Published in Nashville, Tennessee, by Thomas Nelson. Thomas Nelson is a registered trademark of Thomas Nelson, Inc.

Published in association with Blythe Daniel, The Blythe Daniel Agency, Inc., Colorado Springs, CO, www.theblythedanielagency.com.

Thomas Nelson, Inc. titles may be purchased in bulk for educational, business, fund-raising, or sales promotional use. For information, please e-mail SpecialMarkets@ThomasNelson.com.

Stories of individuals who were interviewed for inclusion in this book are used by permission of the persons featured in the stories. Some names have been changed to protect the identity and safety of the story contributor.

Unless otherwise noted, Scripture quotations are from the Holy Bible: New International Version®. © 1973, 1978, 1984 by International Bible Society. Used by permission of Zondervan Publishing House. All rights reserved.

Scripture quotations marked MSG are from *The Message* by Eugene H. Peterson. © 1993, 1994, 1995, 1996, 2000. Used by permission of NavPress Publishing Group. All rights reserved.

Library of Congress Cataloging-in-Publication Data

Kennedy, Kimberley.
    Left at the altar : my story of hope and healing for every woman who has felt the heartbreak of rejection / Kimberley Kennedy.
        p. cm.
    Includes bibliographical references.
    ISBN 978-0-7852-2878-3 (pbk.)
    1. Kennedy, Kimberley. 2. Christian biography—United States. 3. Single women—Religious life. 4. Rejection (Psychology)—Religious aspects—Christianity. I. Title.
BR1725.K435A3 2008
248.8'43—dc22   2008035936

Printed in the United States of America

09 10 11 12 13 RRD 5 4 3 2 1

To Mommy—

the most beautiful example of faith and courage

a woman could have.

You are my heart.

One knows what one has lost,

but not what one may find.

—GEORGE SAND

The Haunted Pool (1851)

Contents

Introduction

Besides death and taxes, rejection may be the most common human experience we face. Whether you are that kid in fifth grade who never got picked for Red Rover or the employee who got passed over for an expected promotion, there is not a person alive who hasn't faced it in some form or another. Still, there is no rejection that can hurt us, in fact cripple us, like the rejection from someone we love. That is as painful as it gets.

Believe me when I tell you that having Diane Sawyer do not one but *three* stories about my sad story on ABC and then *writing a book* about healing from rejection are not what I thought I would be doing at this stage in my life. In fact, rejection was not even in my vocabulary when mine happened. That year I was at the top of my television career, a five o'clock news anchor in Atlanta, and was engaged to the man of my dreams. I was twenty-four hours away from being that woman other women secretly hate: the woman who has it all.

But within a few moments inside St. Luke's Episcopal Church in Atlanta, I learned about rejection the hard way. I got left at the altar. Literally. And as if that weren't horrible enough, being on television only made it a thousand times worse. It took about thirty-six hours for news of my dumping to make it to the morning paper gossip column and radio shows where my radio pals took it upon themselves to give my now-former fiancé a public lynching (which, okay, did make me feel a little better), but still, it was embarrassing and humiliating to deal with such terrible heartache in full public view.

Not long ago there was a story in the news about a woman who also got left at the altar. But instead of wallowing in her self-pity, she turned her wedding reception into a party for the homeless. Just so you know, that was not me. It never in a million years would have occurred to me to put on a happy face and do something so selfless for other people. I am afraid there was not anything noble or redeeming about how I handled my rejection. To be honest, I was pretty awful.

But during that time I got the most unbelievable support and encouragement, not just from my family and friends who loved me, but from people who knew me only from television, strangers I probably never would meet. I kept every single letter I received, and reading them again now for this book reminds me just how much they meant, how much strength and hope they gave me.

The tone of those letters ran the gamut. Some were funny, like the woman who promised to sic her terrier on my former fiancé if she ever ran into him, or poignant, like the scores of women and men who wrote of their own painful rejections. But the words of one woman in particular obviously were planted deep in my mind, waiting to emerge at just the right time. She said, "Use this experience to help others. You're a journalist. You've got the makings of a very interesting story." Now seems to be the right time.

Yes, I am aware that not a lot of people are going to relate to the exact circumstances of my story. I mean, let's be honest, not too many people actually get left at the altar. But if you are in the throes of having your heart broken by someone you love, you will likely see yourself in my story. Rejection is rejection, no matter how it happens.

The good news here is that my story did not end at the church. As you will see, things got worse before they got better. But life did get better. Much better. Those words probably seem hollow to you now—they would have to me at the time—but please read on. This book is for you. My heart aches when I think of all the broken relationships and lingering feelings of hurt, pain, and rejection they leave behind. And even though our friends and loved ones try, it is often hard for people who have not lived it to fully understand. That is why God and I want to tell you this story. I am certainly no professional, but I have had the best training possible. I have lived it. And I not only survived; I thrived. And I can now see that the horrible moment in the church, which felt like the end of the world, was actually a new beginning.

I hope you will consider the following pages my gift to you. From one woman to another. I am going to share with you the most personal details of my life, and I hope you will find some common ground to help you or someone you know. I am also going to share the stories of other women who have been metaphorically "left at the altar," some whom I know, some whom I have met in writing this book. These are women who have been divorced, betrayed, rejected within their marriages, or rejected in the dating world. Their stories, like mine, will make you laugh, make you cry, and most importantly, give you hope.

If you are single, I have a special gift for you too. I am finally going to give some answers about men from men. You are going to hear about rejection from their perspectives: not men who have been rejected, but men who have *done* the rejecting. What these men have to say will likely surprise you and, hopefully, give you some valuable tools as you navigate the murky and often rough waters of dating.

In the spirit of full disclosure, however, I must tell you that this may not be the story you think it is going to be. Yes, I am going to tell you all the humiliating details of what it is like literally to get left at the altar and to lose every ounce of self-respect and self-love you ever had. But this is not a love story about a woman and a man. This is a story about a woman and her God, a God who loved her so much that he allowed a terrible thing to happen to her. Not because he didn't love her but because something much more important was at stake. He had invaluable life lessons for her to learn, lessons that not only would bring her closer to him but also show her in the end that his love is the only love that will never disappoint. Now, *that's* a story!

—KIMBERLEY KENNEDY

One

The End of Forever

We never know the good we have
till constant friends depart
And leave us just with half a life
and half a heart.[1]

—KATHARINE TYNAN HINKSON

It was a beautiful morning that day in late April. Of course, it always seems to be a beautiful day when you are in love. The sky is a little bluer, the birds' chirping sounds a little sweeter, your favorite songs always seem to be on the radio.

But that April day was even more beautiful than all the others because this was the start of my beautiful wedding weekend, the beginning of my life with Lew.

This was the day of the wedding rehearsal, and my home was filled with all the hurried prewedding preparations. Wedding gifts were arriving, friends were coming in from out of town, the phone was ringing, my mom and I were excitedly packing for my honeymoon. In the midst of all that, like Julie Andrews dancing around with those draperies in *The Sound of Music*, I would grab my wedding dress hanging on the armoire and stand in front of the mirror, imagining myself walking down the aisle as Lew gazed at me lovingly from the altar.

I was a grown woman silly in love, and I wanted to remember every single second of this amazing day. This was a story we would tell our children and our grandchildren over and over again.

> I was on top of the world because every minute was inching me closer to him, closer to our being husband and wife.

Anyone who has been a bride knows how intoxicating a time it is before a wedding. As the bride-to-be, you feel as if you are the center of the universe. Everyone is buzzing around you, giggling and happy. Nothing sad from the past is important; all that matters is right now. For my family and me there had been a lot of those sad times, but things finally seemed to be going our way, *my way*, and I just knew that all that sadness was finally behind us.

Of course, the object of all that anticipation was Lew. He was the man I was about to call my "husband." I could not wait to say that. I could not wait to say I was his "wife." And so, as I left home that sunny April afternoon, I was on top of the world because every minute was inching me closer to him, closer to our being husband and wife.

Inside the church was the typical wedding rehearsal scene: the organist asking last-minute questions, the priest wanting to know about a scripture reading, everyone talking and laughing. I was wearing a long cream-colored halter dress that my mom and sister and I had bought on one of our many prewedding shopping trips. It was so pretty, and I remember hoping Lew would think so too.

The church was lovely, aged, and stately, a typical Episcopal church from long ago. It smelled old, which I liked, I guess because it gave off a whiff of permanence and stability, just as a marriage should be. It was so lovely that it occurred to me that, if the flowers somehow never arrived tomorrow, it would be beautiful enough as it was.

And the *joy!* I had never felt such joy. Everyone I loved most in the world was about to be inside this church. I truly was on a love-high, my heart admittedly racing a bit from all the excitement. This was *my* wedding, not my sister's or my friends', *mine.* Don't get me wrong; being a bridesmaid is great and such an honor (I should know; I have had plenty of experience), but finally it was my turn. My turn to get the groom and the happy ending.

Lew was late, but then he was always late, so I wasn't really concerned until a few moments later when his sister came in. In stark contrast to the happy people who had already arrived, she was pale and obviously shaken. She came up to me and said that Lew needed to see me . . . and in that moment I knew. Lew, the priest, and I went into her office. Before Lew said a word, I begged him not to do it, not to say it.

He was clearly distraught, and when he was finally able to speak, he looked directly at me and simply said, "Kimberley, I just can't do it."

I just can't do it. Five little words that would change my life forever.

I have given a lot of thought about how to describe the way I felt at that moment, but I guess anyone who has had a sudden shock or death of a loved one knows how it feels. At first I felt numb, stunned, as if I were having an out-of-body experience. *Did he just tell me he could not go through with our wedding? Surely I had not heard him correctly. I must have misunderstood, or maybe this was not even real. I was just having a nightmare.* But as the numbness wore off, my heart began beating so fast that it must have snapped me back into the horrible reality. He had said it. "I just can't do it." Lew was not going to marry me.

As my body began shaking and my eyes welled up with tears, I could see in his eyes that this time I would not be able to reassure him, that I would not be able to change his mind.

Still, I tried.

Even as I pleaded and begged, I knew it was in vain. I remember looking over at the priest, who clearly had never encountered this kind of thing before, standing there in nearly as much shock as I was, hoping *she* would have the words to fix this, but all she could do was look back at me with this profound sadness.

A thousand thoughts went through my mind. Mostly I just wanted to see my mother.

> *I just can't do it.* Five little words that would change my life forever.

Lew never went out to tell our families and friends that this rehearsal, this wedding, was not going to happen. He left that up to his sister, who also informed those waiting, as I found out later, that they could still join their family at the club for dinner where his unknowing parents were waiting to host the rehearsal dinner. When I learned that, I was stunned and hurt that she was still willing to party while my family, friends, and I were so devastated.

The next night, I also discovered, his family tried to secure the band that was to play at the wedding reception for a gathering at his home for his out-of-town guests. And I should also mention that one of us did go on our glorious honeymoon to the south of France. And he took his brother.

Hazy Memories

My memories of the rest of that night and next day are hazy. We were all in such shock, but my family and friends never skipped a beat. They mobilized in such a way as to comfort me while, unbeknownst to me, canceling the wedding and calling all the guests. I remember thinking that this must be what it would be like at my own funeral. Everyone tiptoeing around, speaking in hushed tones, wondering how this could happen to such a wonderful girl, how no one deserved such a horrible thing.

People brought in food and drinks, and my bridesmaids slept on the floor to be near me. As I sat there sobbing on my sofa in my beautiful, long cream-colored halter dress, one of our family friends, a doctor, gently tried to get me to take a sedative, which I did not want to do. I just did not want a false sense of well-being. It was strange, I know, because most people would have wanted to be knocked out at such a time. But for me it was as if I *wanted* to feel the intense pain I was going through. Maybe it was my brain trying to help me accept what had happened, and the only way to do that was to *feel* it. Still, as hard as I tried to refuse, everyone there tried harder to get me to swallow it; there would be plenty of time for feeling the pain later. So I eventually took their "painkiller."

The most vivid memory I have is the strength of my mother. Sitting there in her wheelchair, her arthritic body bearing the weight of her child's heartache, she was stronger than anyone there. But the hurt in her eyes was profound. Her own life had been racked with pain, emotional and physical, but she will tell you that watching her daughter's heart be broken was the worst pain she ever endured.

My Sister's Story

Let me interrupt Kimberley's story for a moment: I'm Kathleen, Kimberley's younger sister. Unfortunately for me, my memories of that night and the next several days are much clearer than hers. Perhaps I can shed more light on the complete horror of what happened and the unimaginable pain of having to undo Kimberley's beautiful wedding.

It is one thing to be the person who it is actually happening to and quite another to be watching it happen to someone you love. Truth be told, it felt as if it was happening to me too. When you are as close as my sister and I, anything that happens to one happens to the other. When one of us succeeds, we both do. We are proud of each other and share the happiness of our successes. And unfortunately the same is true for our failures and sorrows. I still feel the sting of that horrible day because my heart was left at the altar too.

That being said, let me tell you how that dark day unfolded through our family's eyes. We were so thrilled the day had finally arrived. Kimberley had waited so long for this person to come along. She had been through several long-term relationships, some who even proposed, but this one was different: Lew was *the one*.

So there we were. All gathered at the church for the rehearsal. My family, the bridesmaids, the groomsmen, close friends, the priest, all waiting to get the celebration started. The church was beautiful—a traditional Episcopal church with gorgeous stained-glass windows and old wooden pews. The aisle was long, one of the longest in Atlanta. Our parents were married in the very same church.

Since Lew was late, we decided to get started without him. Mom, our brother, and close friends were sitting on the right side of the aisle, and the bridesmaids began to gather at the front of the church so we could be told where to stand. I looked at my sister and thought she was prettier than I had ever seen her. She looked like a princess, and her smile was radiating a glow that made my heart soar. It is always so wonderful to see the people you love get the happiness they deserve.

As we stood ready for direction from the priest, I noticed Lew's sister walk from the back of the church into the sanctuary. She was wearing no makeup. As she got closer I could see she had cried it off.

She then called out to the wedding party, "May I have everyone's attention?"

At that moment my heart, which only seconds earlier had been soaring, was in the pit of my stomach. The wedding party began sitting down in the pews, not sure what they were about to hear. Had something happened to Lew? Had there been a tragic accident? One thing was evident—the news was not going to be good. Something inside told me (and perhaps it was everything that led up to the wedding) that it was something else. My next thought was, *Where's Kimberley?* When I did not see her, my next thought was to get my mother out of there, to extract her from what she was about to hear. As I stood up to grab Mom's wheelchair, I heard Lew's sister say, "Sit down, Kathleen!"

To that I retorted, "Oh no, I'm not hanging around for this," and proceeded to wheel Mom down the longest aisle in Atlanta. Halfway down, I heard Lew's sister explaining that the wedding was not going to happen, that Lew could not go through with it. It sounded as if she was in a tunnel or speaking over the McDonald's drive-thru speaker. But the next words came out loud and clear: "This is going to be hard on Lew."

And that was when this sister lost her control. *Hard on Lew?* I could not believe what she was saying! What in the world did she mean "hard on Lew"? Surely she was joking. He was the one making the despicable decision to break my sister's heart. He was the one who could have made everything better by keeping his commitment. How was this going to be hard on *him*? Perhaps it was my hormones that were still in turmoil from the baby I had given birth to just two months earlier, but I then proceeded to "let 'er rip," as we say in the South.

"You have *got* to be kidding me! Your family is despicable for allowing this to happen. Imagine how my *sister* feels right now." I am sure God was not too happy with me at that particular moment because I am pretty certain there were some not-so-ladylike things that came out of my mouth. But what I saw next was something I will never forget or forgive. When I turned around to continue our trek out of the church, I realized what was happening had finally sunk in for my mother. Her tiny frame was slumped over in the wheelchair, her face was pale, and she was sobbing. Her baby's heart had been crushed, and now so was hers.

By then I was really angry. My brother took Mom to the car, and I headed off to find my sister and Lew. But as I tried to re-enter the church, two of his brothers blocked my entrance. *Why are they protecting him? Isn't it obvious who is wrong here? You guys seemed to love my sister too; shouldn't you be on our side?* But right or wrong, they were clearly going to protect their brother from this crazy sister who was after him. Finally, after more choice words on my part, they let me in, and I discovered my sister was holed up in the priest's office with Lew. So all of us siblings were standing outside the door, and in no uncertain terms, I told all of them what I thought.

Minutes later my sister opened the door, and I saw her face for the first time: ridden with disbelief, her eyes bloodshot and teary, and her body shaking from the trauma. All I wanted to do was cradle her until this horrible nightmare was over. I grabbed her as if she might collapse and guided her to the car where our brother took over. Standing 6'4", our brother is our rock, confident and strong. But at that moment, he had never felt such a loss of control, torn between conflicting emotions: Should he go fight someone or hold Kimberley closely? He chose the latter, of course, and we took her home where we tried to make it all go away.

The Wake

I like to refer to the following few days as *the wake*. No one really knew what to say. I mean, who had ever been in this situation besides us? Before Kimberley could even get inside the house, the bridesmaids rushed to get her wedding dress and veil that had been hanging on her armoire. No need for her to see that! Once I got inside, all I really wanted to do was sit and hold her, but we only had a few hours to cancel the wedding and reach as many guests by phone as we could. One by one, I called the caterer, the cake designer, the florist, all of whom were so kind and understanding. After a brief pause, without fail, they all said, "Don't worry, we'll take care of it." The cake and the food were donated to homeless shelters; the flowers went to nursing homes. And the band, well, Kimberley already told you that part.

The next day was the day the wedding was *supposed to* have happened, and we all awoke hoping the night before had just been a really bad dream. Of course, it was not. We continued to try to reach as many of those four hundred guests as possible, but inevitably, we could not locate everyone. So I drove downtown to the church and stood on the front steps to deliver the news in person to those who had not heard. Cars pulled up, people got out, dressed for a black tie affair, and looked at me quizzically. The words were so difficult to get out. As the sister of the grieving bride, I couldn't help but describe how brokenhearted Kimberley was and—I am sorry, I couldn't help it—my personal feelings for Lew. Each time, there was confusion and then disbelief. Clearly, no one knew what the proper thing to say in that situation was, but most simply said they were sorry.

Aftermath

As for the wedding presents, my mom and a close friend took care of them in the following days as we all continued to go about our duties like church mice, trying to be respectful of the grieving girl in the next room. All the while, our hearts were breaking along with hers.

Let me remind you that my sister is a public personality. She has been on television in Atlanta for years. And if you could see her, you most likely would find her to be someone you would like to know, kind and thoughtful, intelligent and capable, the kind of person you joyfully would welcome into your living room or around your kitchen table. She is extremely likable, mostly because she truly does care about people. She has engrained herself in the community, serving on charity boards, making innumerable speeches, many to young people. She has even rocked AIDS and crack babies at the hospital.

For these reasons, those in the media who knew Kimberley felt compelled to defend her honor. And so the media storm began. Top-40 radio talked about the wretched groom who did the unthinkable. One station, where her close friend was the morning deejay, wrote a song about what a horrible person Lew was, and played it over and over again. The syndicated radio host Neal Boortz solicited callers' thoughts on the disgraceful man named Lew.

Though it was comforting to Kimberley to know she was loved, the embarrassment was more than she could take. That is why we whisked her off to our favorite beach in hopes that the warmth and sunshine and a piña colada would melt the pain. It didn't.

Those are my personal memories of those awful few days, but as you will see as Kimberley's story unfolds, she survived it all . . . as we all knew she would, but it took a while. Boy, did it take a while!

Images and Fragrances

Kathleen is right. It did take a while, probably because the shock and pain were so intense. But my sister's recollections, so strong even today, show you how hurt we all were.

Anyway, you should also know that Lew never called to check on me. By Monday, word had gotten out that I had been left at the altar, and, as Kathleen said, it became great fodder for the morning and afternoon radio shows. While I certainly got the better end of the gossip, it was humiliating for me, and I am sure it was embarrassing for my family. When the newspaper called for a quote, my family decided it was time to get me out of town. I know it was for the best, but being with my mother, my sister, and a bridesmaid was not what I had been expecting to do that week. All I could think of was that I should be on my honeymoon, that I should be with Lew.

I do have some vivid images in my mind of that day, including my postpartum sister yelling things at my fiancé that should never have been said in a church, the grief-stricken face of my younger brother, the strength of my mother, friends on the phone canceling my beautiful wedding, bridesmaids sleeping on my living-room floor. I don't think of those images much anymore, and I rarely incorporate them into my verbal story. I think that is because the hurt of my family and friends was so intense that to conjure them up brings back pain I would rather not remember.

> The smell of fresh flowers . . . waiting for me like a memorial at a funeral when I arrived back home.

But the one image I cannot suppress, even today, is not really an image at all. It is the smell of fresh flowers. My house had been filled with flowers that morning before the wedding. And of course, they were waiting for me like memorials at a funeral when I arrived back home that evening, and to this day I cannot smell gardenias without feeling sad.

Two

The Chapters of My Life

I know that love is blind,
but does it have to be deaf and dumb too?

—AUTHOR UNKNOWN

I have told my story so many times that it usually feels as if I am talking about somebody else, except, of course, on those PMS days when I remember it was me and feel sad. I tell it for two reasons: one, a lot of people heard about it and are curious for details; and two, I want the listener to know that at my age I have at least gotten really close to getting married.

The response is predictable. It begins with amazement, since very few people actually *know* someone who has been left at the altar, and it ends with that look of pity since now they do. And I find that, contrary to most good storytellers, I do not have to take liberty with the facts to make it interesting. No, in this case what actually happened is a good story on its own.

To really understand the story, though, you need to know how I got to that night at the altar, how my past, particularly my college and young adult years, contributed to what happened. I would love to be able to tell you that I am completely blameless in this terrible event, but I think we both know that would not be true. No, I contributed all right, but that's something, unfortunately, I can only now understand in hindsight.

Today I think of my life in four chapters—some shorter, some longer, some fun and easy, some sad and difficult:

1. Childhood to junior year in college

2. Junior year to Lew

3. Lew

4. After Lew

Simple, compartmentalized, controllable, the fall and redemption.

Childhood to Junior Year in College

My younger sister and brother and I grew up in a traditional, all-American household. My mom was a homemaker, my dad an airline pilot. My parents were a beautiful, bright, and sparkly couple whom everybody loved and who always made me proud. We lived on a cattle ranch in a one-caution-light town, an hour and a half south of Atlanta, where my grandfather, a very successful businessman, had retired: lots of land for kids to be kids, Cecil's General Store just down the road, the kind of place where you never locked your doors.

We all were active in our little Presbyterian church in the nearby town. My parents instilled in us good old-fashioned values, such as respect and responsibility and

> It was a perfect way to begin life, I'd have to say.

the importance of taking care of people who were not as fortunate as we were. As kids, we were involved in all the things you might expect: piano, ballet, Little League, horseback riding, golf, and tennis. But somewhere around thirteen, my mom said it was time to figure out which one of those things I had a passion for and zero in on that. Instead of letting me be mediocre at a lot of things, she wisely decided it would be better for me to be really good at one.

I chose tennis, and she was right. What I learned by having a goal, working hard at it, and then excelling at it were important life lessons that would serve (no pun intended) me well. Becoming really good at tennis gave me an incredible sense of confidence and a firm belief that, if you want something badly enough, you can get it, but only if you work hard and never give up. The premise held for a long time.

Between tennis practice, matches, and tournaments, I was a regular teenager: good student, student body treasurer, Beta Club president, senior favorite, editor of the newspaper, and Upson County's Junior Miss. And boys? I went to the proms and dances with boy "friends," but I was never boy-crazy like so many of my friends at that age. Boys were okay; I just had too much else going on, too many plans for the future to give them a whole lot of thought. No, giving them a lot of thought would come much later.

It was a perfect way to begin life, I'd have to say. But the best part about growing up in the Kennedy household was that I always felt loved. Safe and loved. Protected, nurtured, supported, invincible.

Junior Year to Lew

It is too bad we all have to grow up and learn that nothing is ever *truly* perfect. And it is too bad we cannot always learn it in small increments, instead of through the tsunami that hit my junior year in college. That was the year my mother's rheumatoid arthritis made its major assault, knocking her off her feet, literally. She had been diagnosed with the disease the year I was born and had lived fairly normally with it for nineteen years, so this took us all by surprise.

Perhaps it hit my dad harder than anyone else, and he coped with it in a way that pulled the rug out from under all of us and our once-ideal family. He left Mom later that year. He would probably say that he did not leave us kids, just Mom, but he did. He would come and get my little brother on occasional weekends when he was not flying, but he never offered to come and help out at all or to support Mom or us in her now-mounting doctor visits and hospital stays, although he did support us financially. It must have been a very frightening prospect, being the oldest child with a sick mom and two younger siblings, because I told him that if he left us, I would never speak to him again. I don't think he believed me, but I meant it. And for seventeen years I did not speak to my dad.

My final two years in college were tough. Thankfully, I had chosen a small, women's liberal arts college outside Atlanta, Agnes Scott, because I ended up driving home every Friday afternoon and driving back to school late on Sunday night nearly every weekend. My mother and I had always been incredibly close, but when her illness hit so hard, it bound us together even tighter. There was no way I was going to allow her to go through that and the loss of her husband alone. I also went home every week to make sure my siblings, especially my ten-year-old brother, had some sense of normalcy in their lives. It didn't hit me until years later that I never mourned the loss of my dad in my own life. I guess there was just too much else to worry about.

Fast-forward through my twenties and into my thirties, and my family managed to right ourselves after my dad left and

> Anytime there is *stuff* in your past, it is impossible for it not to shape your future.

learned to cope with Mom's progressing illness. Once you accept an illness such as arthritis as a way of life, you just deal with it the best way you can. Do I wish it hadn't happened or that my dad had been there to support us, even if he wasn't married to Mother anymore? Of course. But we did it. I did it. And I think we are all better people for it.

The only problem with this Lifetime movie scenario is that anytime there is *stuff* in your past, it is impossible for it not to shape your future, particularly how you deal with new *stuff*. The abandonment issues I took on from my dad's leaving is a no-brainer. But strangely enough, I believe what I learned on the tennis court ended up having more to do with my response to the things that were to happen than anything else. Set a goal, work hard, and never give up. Rely on yourself. Maintain control. All good lessons when it comes to sports, but not so good when it comes to love.

To say I was a control freak most of my life would be dead-on. I have actually been in love with control, intoxicated by it. It is a powerful feeling to believe you are not only controlling your own life but the lives of the people you care about, making them do the things you think they should be doing (with the best intentions, of course), orchestrating the world around you like a conductor with a baton. Yep, that was me. And quite a mess I made of things, I must admit.

In my own defense, though, let me just say that I think my becoming a control freak was inevitable. The firstborn in any family tends to be the one who likes to run things. And then when my family blew up, my mom got sick, and my dad left, my being in control became necessary. Combine that with the "set a goal, work hard, never give up" mantra tennis had instilled in me, and you can see how I got there. When Lew came along and I knew I wanted to marry him, I just believed I could control him straight to the altar. And even after the rehearsal night disaster, I *still* thought I could get it done. I was just that good.

Lew

Lew and I had met two years earlier on a blind date. And I swore that if this one didn't work out, it would be my last. It was not as if I had been on some massive hunt for a husband. Quite the contrary. I was devoted to my career in television and had spent my twenties pulling every conceivable shift. And believe me, working nights, weekends, and early mornings is not exactly conducive to a great social life. Besides, I

was never one of those women who subscribed to *Bride* magazine. I just
was not desperate to get married. I was willing to wait for the right one,
and at thirty-three I found him. That "final" blind date turned out to
be a winner.

My first impression of Lew was that I was probably taller in my
heels than he was. When you are five feet nine, your first impression
tends to be about height. But after we sat down, he seemed to get
taller. My mom actually remembers my calling her and saying that he
was *kind of* cute, in a preppy sort of way, but definitely interesting. On
that first date, I discovered that Lew had a great education and obviously a very bright mind. He had attended college on a golf scholarship
and was athletic. We were in the same industry—he was in the radio
business—and he had never been married or had children. And to my
delight, we shared the same sense of humor. We laughed at the same
things and made each other laugh. Oh yes, I was definitely intrigued.

It was not long before I discovered something else: we got along
great. We just enjoyed being together. Unlike most men, Lew did not
seem to need to spend a lot of time with his buddies. He was content
to be with me. In the coming weeks and months, I was to learn other
things that were important to me too. He was close to his family, as
was I. He had a strong work ethic and great ambition. He was always
generous. And he became my biggest fan and supporter. But just three
months after we started dating, I began doing what women in love
usually do—demanding to know where this relationship was headed.

Let me say this right off the bat: men don't generally like it when
you ask them where a relationship is headed. And that was certainly
the case with Lew. He was used to being in charge at work, and he

wanted it that way in his private life too. In the end we both agreed things were great, and Lew suggested we continue on as we were and let things evolve on their own.

Unfortunately, that did not hold me off for long. Back then I was not so patient. And I have always been a goal setter. Besides, we were such a perfect match it seemed obvious to me that we should get married. So like a heat-seeking missile, I zeroed in on my target. After a year, I gave him a choice; it was an ultimatum: fish or cut bait. He decided to fish, and we got engaged.

Now, I wish I could tell you here that it was a magical, romantic proposal, but that wasn't the kind of guy Lew was. And not only that but the proposal came right after a pretty heated argument over whether we were going to get married or not. He had already bought the *beautiful* diamond engagement ring he produced, which settled me inside, since he had obviously gotten it on his own, without my help. That told me in a tender, yet hard-fought way, that he truly did want the same thing I did: for us to be together.

> Men don't generally like it when you ask them where a relationship is headed.

That part of the story will come as a surprise to my family and friends who never knew the circumstances of Lew's proposal. We announced our engagement to them like any couple in love would do. That night we celebrated with our brothers and sisters. Everybody was happy and hopeful, and even Lew seemed genuinely relieved that we had finally put permanence in our relationship. I know I was. This was the man for whom I had waited my whole life. Life with him was going to be a great adventure, and I could not wait.

Not long after our engagement, Lew and I set out on the mission of finding our home. We would spend our weekends driving around Atlanta, looking at houses, and many hours with a Realtor, walking through the ones we liked. It was such a fun time and so affirming to me just how perfect Lew and I were for one another. The kitchens I liked, he liked; the bathrooms I hated, he hated; the brick, the colors, the yards, the neighborhoods—we really did agree on pretty much everything. And when we finally found the perfect home, he bought it immediately. He moved in, and we both began getting ready for me to live there after the wedding.

But it was getting to *when* that wedding would take place that would set into motion the entire episode of my ultimate rejection. Immediately after our engagement, I tried to set a wedding date, which still does not seem odd to me since that's what engaged people do. A friend later reminded me that, when the news of our engagement appeared in the *Atlanta Journal-Constitution*'s gossip column, my quote about when the big day would be was: "I'm thinking sooner; he's thinking later." How prophetic! I was hoping to be married in the fall; he suggested Christmas. So Christmas it was.

My mom, my sister, and I began the planning: the hunt for the dress, the flowers, the color theme for the reception, the food, the band. The printed invitations had even arrived when Lew announced he wanted to wait until spring. *Spring? My bridesmaids are going to carry white muffs instead of flowers; we cannot wait until spring!* Needless to say I was upset. Anyone who has planned a wedding knows that changing the date so close to the event is not easy to do. But it was not really the muffs or the logistics of changing the wedding particulars that concerned me. Obviously this was a man with cold feet. Still, despite the hurt, the tears, and the arguing, he never once said he did not want to get married. He simply wanted to wait. I guess in my mind I believed, as long as we eventually were going to be married, that was all that mattered. Printing four hundred new invitations and rescheduling the caterer were not such big deals when you are talking about a lifetime.

This time we decided on an April wedding, which would be exactly two years after we met. But even pushing back the date did not appease Lew after a while. He was soon finding fault with me and everything else. Small things became gigantic issues. We argued incessantly, something we had never done before. He insisted on a prenuptial agreement, which I agreed to sign, despite my attorney's very strong advice not to sign it. I now wonder if Lew was hoping that by insisting I sign a prenup, it might force *me* to call off the wedding. At the time, however, I truly felt that he was simply anxious, as any groom would be, and that once he said, "I do," we would be fine. So I persevered, plowed on, and continued to plan our wedding and new life.

I should, however, have known we really were in trouble the day before the rehearsal when we went to get our marriage license, and he would not get out of the car. Not a good sign. Again and again I assured him that it was just nerves, that he knew this was right, and that we were going to be happy. Finally he agreed, we got out of the car, and we soon had the license in hand, but by then my anxiety level was matching his own.

Right about now you are probably thinking, *How could anybody with half a brain and one iota of self-respect not give him back his engagement ring and call the whole thing off herself?* That is an easy one to explain: I was in love. It is as simple as that.

After Lew

The final chapter of my life is all about recovery from the loss of Lew and how God helped me to put my life back together. It is by far the best part of the story.

Three

Suspended in Time

There's nothing wrong with grief.
After all, grief is simply evidence that
you loved someone.[1]

—THE GRIEF ADJUSTMENT GUIDE

Remembering how I felt the exact moment I knew Lew was not going to marry me was like remembering where you were on September 11. Time goes by, but you can recall in vivid detail precisely what you felt when you heard the news. It's as if your body has a shut-off valve to protect you from truly comprehending the magnitude of what you are experiencing until you are able to process it.

It begins with a numbness. But as numbness usually does, mine quickly wore off, and I had to face the painful reality that I wasn't getting married because the man I loved did not want to marry me. Someone might as well have come in and told me Lew had been hit by a bus because it could not have felt any worse if he had. In fact, if I think about it, it might have been easier to handle if he had. Not that I would

27

have wanted him to be hit by a bus, but I had to live with the fact that it was no accident that prevented us from being together. Lew *chose* to leave me. He *rejected* me. And, boy, the hurt in that.

Autopilot

At the risk of sounding overly dramatic, it really was as if Lew had died. We have all been there in the hours and days after someone has passed away. You mourn while people mobilize and bring food and comfort. They organize what needs to be organized. They talk in whispers. Things move at a hectic pace while you operate on autopilot, just going through the motions but emotionally disconnected.

> I had been dumped. And the whole world knew.

For example, for a long time I had no idea what happened to my wedding dress. When I left home the night of the rehearsal, it was hanging on my armoire. I never saw it when I got home from the church.

However, I do have a vague recollection of my mom and her friend hauling all my wedding gifts to Mom's house and getting them back to the senders, all accompanied by a card explaining what had happened. Well, not really what happened. *That* note would have said that the horrible Lew had made the unconscionable, last-minute, worst-minute-possible decision not to marry her daughter—the most deserving, wonderful girl on earth. Instead, Mom's note simply stated that the wedding between Kimberley and Lew had not taken place as planned, but thank you very much for your gift anyway. As if anybody who sent a gift needed a note to tell them that. I was so mired in self-pity I couldn't imagine anybody who had not heard about it. I had been dumped. And the whole world knew.

The Flip Side

The flip side of all this, of course, is that while I was rejected by one man, an army of people showed up to demonstrate how much I was loved. There is no way to overstate the love and support I got from my family and friends. They came, they called, and they listened ad nauseam to how heartbroken I was. I probably will never know everything they did to get me through those first few days and weeks.

One of my bridesmaids even offered to come live with me for a while, obviously concerned that I might try to put myself out of my misery. Even as miserable as I was, I never once considered that, although at the time it was pretty difficult to think of a reason why I shouldn't.

In any case, people can only hang on for so long. Eventually their lives had to go on, even if mine wasn't, and so the food stopped coming, and the people and the calls thinned out. Sad as it felt then, it was time for me to be by myself because at some point I had to face, head-on, what happened, deal with it, and get on with my life. I just could not do that with a house full of people.

To Sleep, Perchance to Dream

It was, however, the *dealing-with-it* part that I found to be tough. That is because my mourning took on a life of its own. I was so sad and so hurt in the beginning that I could not get out of bed. I mean, why should I? What was there to get up for anyway? And when I did wake up, my first thought was always, *Please, God, let this all have been a bad dream.* All the day had to offer me was the tortured reminder of being rejected by Lew. And besides, there was something safe about being asleep. Like that old Skylark song from the seventies says, "Sleep's the only freedom that she knows."[2] When I was asleep, I found a peace I couldn't find when I was awake.

I remember looking in the mirror one day and not recognizing myself. The pain, the hopelessness in my eyes, the paleness of my skin, the hair that needed brushing, all had taken the place of that happy, confident person I used to be. A sure sign I had given in to my depression was that I quit painting my toenails; after all, who now would be *seeing* my toenails? And going back to work? Unthinkable! How in the world could I ever muster up the strength—the courage—to go back on the air in front of all of Atlanta with everyone knowing what had happened to me? Nothing during that time mattered except my heartbreak. It was as if the world had stopped spinning and I was left in a suspended state of despair.

There were actually two endeavors I did enjoy. The first was blaming, hating, and yelling at God. I was so angry at him for *allowing* this terrible thing to happen and destroy my life. The only Bible verse that made any sense to me at all was the one where Jesus is on the cross, and he says, "My God, my God, why have you forsaken me?" (Matt. 27:46). I felt that God had totally abandoned me when he knew better than anybody that I deserved to have something good happen. In my mind, I had been a *good* person, a *faithful* churchgoer; God should have intervened and *made* Lew marry me.

The other endeavor I really enjoyed was self-torture. All I could think about, all I *wanted* to think about, was Lew. I mourned the past: I reflected on every happy moment we had shared. Over and over again, like hitting the rewind button on the VCR to replay your favorite part of a home movie. I thought about how we met, places we had gone, things that had made us laugh. I mourned the present: I missed the presence of him. I missed his coming through the door, his take on things, all the fun things we were not doing. And I mourned the future that now would not be: decorating our Christmas tree, the kindergarten play, family vacations to the beach, growing old together. The more I thought about it, the more I cried. All of those images in my mind make me wonder how I ever survived the weight of it. I was grieving the past, present, and future.

> How in the world could I ever . . . go back on the air in front of all of Atlanta with everyone knowing what had happened to me?

Not Alone

When I was a little girl, my parents used to call me Sarah Bernhardt. For those of you too young to get the reference, Sarah Bernhardt was possibly the greatest stage actress who has ever lived. What my parents meant when they called me that was that I could, on occasion, be overly dramatic. Okay, perhaps on more than one occasion.

But when I tell you that I actually *grieved* after Lew left me, I do not think I am overstating my state of mind. Let me make a quick point here, however. I am well aware that, in the whole scheme of things that can happen to a person, being left at the altar is bad, but it is not as bad as a lot of other things, such as the death of a child or dealing with cancer. But the blow of someone you love rejecting you does make you *feel* as if it is. And so I *mourned* that man just as I would have had he died.

> You are not alone.
> You are not some
> freak of nature.

In my discussions through the years with other women who have been rejected, I have discovered that that reaction was not unique to me. In fact, grieving the person who has rejected you seems to be universal. I have had women tell me they felt . . .

- flattened
- shattered
- as if their hearts had been literally torn from their bodies
- that life no longer had meaning
- that they could see no future for themselves
- as if they wanted to die

And in response many tell me they . . .

- immersed themselves in only the happy memories of the relationship
- listened to sad songs or watched sad movies over and over again

- stopped eating, making themselves physically sick

- began overeating to try to ease the pain with food

- began drinking or abusing prescription drugs to feel better

- isolated themselves from the world, including family and friends, preferring to wallow in and prolong their grief, rather than even try to move forward

Therapists tell me they hear the exact same things when clients come in to get help dealing with the *death* of someone they loved. The exact same things.

So here's the deal: you need to know that you are not alone. You are not some freak of nature. What you are feeling is very real. But before we can get you back out there living your life, you need to understand the stages you will likely go through. Do not let them scare you. They do not have to last long. In fact, therapists tell me some of them may overlap one another. But to even *start* to move forward, you may need to work through them all. How long it takes is up to you.

Road Map to Recovery

Lucky for us, there is actually a road map to grief recovery. It is based on that groundbreaking book that came out in 1969 called *On Death and Dying* (notice the "death" analogy), written by an internationally renowned psychiatrist, Dr. Elisabeth Kübler-Ross. Having been asked to write a book about death and dying, Dr. Kübler-Ross spent two and half years talking to people who were terminally ill and listening to their stories. What she discovered was a definable cycle of emotions that nearly all dying patients go through. In her book, she coined the now-famous "Five Stages of Grief."

Today, counselors and therapists use those five stages to help people who have faced other traumatic events, such as rape or *rejection.*

See if you can see your own state of mind in these five stages. I know I did.

Stage 1: Denial and Isolation

There is often such shock at hearing you are being rejected that the first thing you do is deny it. Denial hit me hard as I stood there in the priest's office, hearing Lew tell me he could not marry me. But for me this period didn't last more than a day or so past those first forty-eight hours sobbing on my sofa uncontrollably.

Stage 2: Anger

In my story this was not anger at Lew; it was anger at God. I was so mad at him for allowing Lew to leave me at the altar that I actually remember screaming at him and telling him I hated him. That stage of anger did last a while.

Stage 3: Bargaining

I so wanted to marry Lew, even after he did such a dishonorable thing, that I had myself believing he really *wanted* to eventually marry me, so I bargained with myself that if I could just be understanding enough and forgiving enough and loving enough, he would do it. That stage lasted only until I could see that none of it was going to work.

Stage 4: Depression

When I finally faced the fact that Lew and I were not going to get married . . . ever, then the depression sank in. And, boy, did it sink in. This lasted, as you have heard, for quite a while, even causing me to make a decision to leave a very good-paying job and to get so emotionally stressed-out that my body reacted with disease. There was a lot of sleeping during this stage. I isolated myself, and complete hopelessness set in. This was also when I just *knew* I would never be happy again.

Stage 5: Acceptance

Oh, the beginning of the rebirth! Acceptance. For me, that's when my reliance on God began to take hold. It was when I realized I could not control my life or anyone else's and when I finally gave the reins to God to let him turn my life around, inwardly and outwardly. Glimmers of hope turned into embers during this phase. Life began to look hopeful and promising once again.

The Valley of Grief

While it is true that there are five basic stages of grief, those stages can be broken into many other phases and intermediate steps of loss and recovery. These include the first experiences of shock, numbness, denial, emotional outbursts, anger, fear, searchings, and disorganization followed by the deeper feelings of panic, loneliness, depression, guilt, and isolation. Then on to experiences that reflect adjustment to grief—new relationships, new strengths, new patterns, hope, affirmation, and helping others.

The following chart illustrates these typical experiences. You might like to work your way through this grief chart by focusing on your own loss experiences. You can make a photocopy of this chart so you can write on it easily. Then do these steps:

- ~~Cross out~~ experiences you remember *already having.*
- <u>Underline</u> experiences you're *currently experiencing.*
- Place a check (✔) beside experiences you *haven't had yet.*

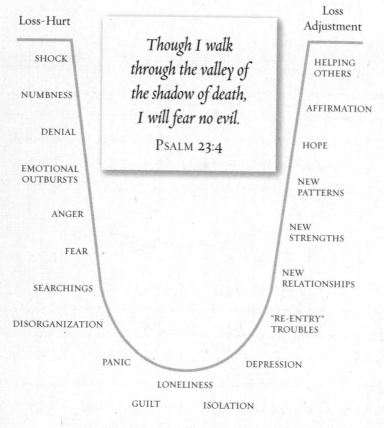

Loss-Hurt

Loss Adjustment

Though I walk through the valley of the shadow of death, I will fear no evil.

PSALM 23:4

SHOCK

NUMBNESS

DENIAL

EMOTIONAL OUTBURSTS

ANGER

FEAR

SEARCHINGS

DISORGANIZATION

PANIC

LONELINESS

GUILT   ISOLATION

HELPING OTHERS

AFFIRMATION

HOPE

NEW PATTERNS

NEW STRENGTHS

NEW RELATIONSHIPS

"RE-ENTRY" TROUBLES

DEPRESSION

Taken from *The Grief Adjustment Guide*[3]

Searching

Just because you have lost someone in your life, it does not mean that he disappears from your heart and mind. And most people who have been left behind, even when they are working hard to move forward, find themselves searching for the one they have lost wherever they go, whether consciously or subconsciously.

For instance, you are walking through the mall when you catch a glimpse of a man in the crowd. He walks as *he* did, he holds his head slightly cocked to one side as *he* did, he is wearing Dockers and loafers as *he* did, or his hair and build from your vantage point look just like *him*. And your heart jumps into your throat. Then you realize, sadly, it is not him.

Sometimes a rejected lover goes searching for a lost love on purpose. You drive past his house, hoping to see him. You *just drop by* old haunts the two of you once shared, hoping to *accidentally* bump into him. You are constantly watching for his car on streets where you know he travels regularly.

Searching. Searching. Always searching . . . for the one you have lost. It is normal. You are not weird or strange. It is a usual, predictable part of working through your loss.

Yet searching is a part of denial. And as long as you are still searching for him, you have not given up the idea that you might get him back. You believe in the recesses of your mind and

> Searching. Searching. Always searching . . . for the one you have lost. It is normal.

heart that there is still hope for you and him to be together. After all, you think, he did not *really* reject you out of hand; he was just temporarily upset, and he actually wants to come back to you.

Give up the search! Unfortunately, even if you find him, more than likely it will be a more painful encounter than helpful. Try to move on. It is the healthy thing to do. Not easy, but healthy.

Here It Comes Again

Those of us who have been left at the altar or left behind for other reasons know that grieving a loss is not a one-time-for-all-time thing. Just because you have worked your way through the grief of losing your boyfriend or fiancé or even your husband doesn't mean you have grieved for him in each of the other varied roles he played in your life. And this can blindside you at unexpected moments as Grief raises its ugly head over and over again. Tears and bouts of depression may overwhelm you unexpectedly like waves washing over the beach.

For instance, perhaps your fiancé helped you prepare your income taxes each year. When April rolls around next year, and it is time to file your taxes, Grief may pay you a visit again when he is not there to fill that role he has played for you in the past. And you have to find someone else to fill in that slot in your life.

Or, perhaps, when something went wrong with your car, he was the one you called to fix it. So several months down the road, when your car battery goes dead, you may automatically pick up your cell phone to call him, only to realize, once again, that he is not there to fill that role as usual. And Grief knocks on the door of your mind as a recurring unwelcome guest.

Until you have encountered all the roles he played and have managed to replace him in those roles in your life, your grieving is not finished. So do not be caught off guard when you suddenly find yourself crying when you have to do something alone that you have been doing with him.

One helpful thing you might do to anticipate Grief's visits is to make a list of all the roles the one you have lost played in your life. Then, perhaps, you will not be so surprised when Grief comes knocking at those times. Was he tennis partner, plumber, escort to business functions, confidant, Valentine, your Santa Claus, New Year's Eve date, the one who balanced your checkbook, or the other half of your duet? Try to list as many different roles as you can, and use the list to think ahead about what might be coming up. If you are expecting it, perhaps the blow will not be quite so severe.

> Until you have encountered all the roles he played and have managed to replace him in those roles in your life, your grieving is not finished.

Sharon and Bill

Let me tell you a story about a woman we will call Sharon, who, as I am writing this, is right in the middle of the grief of her rejection. She is feeling about as hopeless as anyone I have ever known.

Sharon is a successful forty-three-year-old businesswoman. She has been divorced for about twelve years and is, frankly, surprised to find herself still single after all that time, particularly because people are always telling her what a catch she is.

Finally Sharon met someone. And as luck would have it, he lived not only in her same apartment building, but on her floor just a few doors down. That made things exciting in the beginning. He would leave cute notes on her door, they would take impromptu walks to get coffee, and eventually they would cook dinners together.

Sharon says she became smitten with—let's call him Bill—not only because they were having so much fun together but also because it was so refreshing to be *pursued*. He called her and e-mailed her often, he met her friends, and he went and watched her tennis matches. And after she underwent some fairly major surgery, Bill came and brought flowers and even rubbed her feet.

For about four months this went on, with Sharon and Bill spending more and more time together. She says she knew she was really falling for him when she could feel herself letting her guard down and becoming vulnerable. She was certainly falling in love.

Then it happened. Sharon had to be rushed to the hospital for a complication from her surgery. Bill had been out of town, and Sharon's friends called him immediately to let him know she was in trouble. They called and called and e-mailed. No response.

By Monday morning, Sharon, now back at home, got worried about Bill since she had not heard from him. Maybe he had been in a car accident or was sick or his parents were sick. So she called him. When he finally called her back, she said he was as "cold as ice," "disinterested," and acted as if he did not care. Sharon said it was so weird; it was as if Bill had "flipped a switch" and become someone else. What happened to the guy who rubbed her feet?

A week later, Bill went to Sharon's apartment and proceeded to tell her that he never had had feelings for her, that there was no spark between them, and that he was tired of faking it. And the reason he never went to the hospital was because, and I quote here, "On a scale of one to ten you care for me an eight. I care for you a one or two." Sharon broke down right in front of him.

Sharon says she is feeling a profound sense of rejection. She is in complete depression over the ending of this relationship, particularly because it was as if one minute he was really crazy about her and the next, he wasn't. She really was beginning to see a permanent future for the two of them. And, oh yeah, this all happened the week before her forty-third birthday.

Sharon, as I did, feels as if God abandoned her, that he could have brought a *nice* man to her door instead of the one who lived down the hall. She wonders if God is punishing her because she is divorced. She has begged him to let her get hit by a truck, to "take her out." She truly feels she has no reason to live. She is forty-three years old with no husband and no children and feels as if she will never have either. In Sharon's heart there is no tomorrow.

Future Stories

Future story is a term coined by a well-known pastoral counselor named Andrew D. Lester. He first used it in his book *Hope in Pastoral Care and*

> It is not the past or even the present causing her lack of hope; it's the patient's . . . lack of a "future story."

Counseling, which was written to other pastoral counselors to guide them in their care of people who are suffering a lack of hope. I first heard about it in a Bible study, and did it ever resonate with me.

Lester's premise is this: while most counselors and therapists tend to focus on what is happening *currently* in a patient's life or on what happened in her *past,* the thing they should really be focusing on is her *future.* It is not the past or even the present causing her lack of hope; it's the patient's view of the future or, as he calls it, the lack of a "future story." Here is what Lester says:

Given our constant projections into the future and the investment of hope in specific content, it is not surprising to learn that one cause of despair is the loss of a future story. This is particularly so when the loss is sudden and traumatic, as in the unexpected death of a loved one, an announcement out of the blue that a spouse wants a divorce, or failing to get admitted to graduate school. A major change in circumstances significantly alters a future story.

Some people experience the beginning of despair when they reach the end of a future story in which they were extensively invested, and no other future story has been put in its place.[4]

Lester believes that, in order for counselors and therapists to lead their patients out of this despair, they need to help those patients shape *new* future stories. He says, "From the beginning we need to communicate our assumption that talking about the future and hope is as natural and as important to the healing process as talking about the past and present."[5]

Back to Sharon

Right now Sharon has no future story. Scratch that. Sharon does have a future story; it is just not a very good one in her view. She sees her future as being alone and unloved. What she must start trying to see, and she may need professional help to do this, is a future where she is living the amazing life God promised her, where she is happy and fulfilled. Believe me, I spent a lot of time where Sharon is now, feeling hopeless and unable to construct a future story for myself that had any promise. But when you can begin to do that, the grieving will gradually go away.

If you really get down to it, you aren't just grieving the person who has rejected you. You are also grieving the romanticized future you had built in your mind that included the two of you together. The carriage has turned back into a pumpkin, the horses have become rats once again, and Cinderella is grieving the loss of her prince.

There is still an amazing future waiting for you. It just does not include him. And the sooner you can get yourself to the *acceptance stage*, the sooner you will be able to stop grieving and begin building a new "future story" of your own. There probably is a prince out there, just a *different* prince, and he has a glass slipper that fits only you.

Four

More Than Worthy

No one can make you feel inferior without your permission.

—Eleanor Roosevelt

Another thing I really enjoyed doing during my period of mourning and grief was beating myself up—not for being unable or unwilling to see what was coming, despite the obvious signs. No, this was all about what was *wrong* with me. It's strange. When you have been dumped, you never once think the problem was his. Instead, every tiny insecurity you have about yourself springs to life and overwhelms your thinking. *What an awful, undesirable person I must be to have caused a man to do such an unthinkable thing. Was I too old, too skinny, too fat, not smart enough, too smart? What was it about me that he didn't want to spend his life with anyway?* I hated myself so much that I began to wonder why Lew had ever loved me at all.

I have come to find out that I was not alone in feeling all that self-hate. Nearly every single woman I have talked with about her rejection felt exactly the same way. A woman named Liz had been dating a man for nearly a year when he suddenly called her on the phone (you would think he could have done it in person after being together that long) and said he did not think it was going to work out between them. She really thought she was going to marry this guy; she had given her entire heart to him and revealed things to him about herself she had never revealed to any other man. Her family and friends loved him. Liz tells me she was devastated, flattened. And rather than be angry at *him,* she spent weeks and weeks beating herself up, wondering what *she* had done.

"All of a sudden," she said, "he doesn't think I'm great. And if he doesn't think I'm great, I must not be."

The Bachelor

There is a popular show on television called *The Bachelor,* and once again, in the spirit of full disclosure, I have to admit I have watched it. (Okay, maybe I do watch it every week, but that's beside the point.) I feel guilty watching it, my being a modern woman and all, but there is just something about it that makes me want to tune in. And apparently the same goes for a lot of other people since the network keeps renewing it season after season. On paper, it does not sound like the type of television show any self-respecting, new-millennial woman would consider appointment TV. The premise sounds outdated, old-fashioned even, but for millions of viewers it works.

The idea is that a handsome, successful bachelor goes looking for a wife among twenty-five women who do whatever they can to get his attention and affection. And by the end of each episode, they hope to receive from him a rose. By the end of the series, they hope to become the last woman standing, ultimately winning the bachelor's heart. It's amazing to watch a woman vie for the attention of a man she doesn't even know but somehow *knows* that he is the one with whom she wants to spend her life.

On one episode, women sang "The Star-Spangled Banner," challenged the buff bachelor to push-ups, and literally did backflips. I am not kidding, one woman—a *medical* student, no less—did backflips to get him to notice her. Apparently, I am not the only one bewildered by the continued success of *The Bachelor* because the Associated Press did an entire piece on the subject. The writer concluded that the female contestants represent all the anxieties women in general have about themselves, especially the anxiety that they will never land that someone special. According to the article, the show is popular among women because we want to see how others deal with rejection.[1]

True enough. The show spends a great deal of time with a camera pointed in the anguished face of the discarded bachelorette as she drives away in a limousine from the bachelor who just rejected her. It is so sad that each time, you just want to reach through the screen and take the wounded woman in your arms and console her, mostly because you have been there and know how she feels.

Finally, though, there is always the happy-ending part of the show. Who isn't a sucker for a happy ending? Despite the rejection that goes on week after week, you know there will be a payoff in the end, and the bachelor will eventually choose *someone* who will see all her dreams come true.

Not everyone, however, is buying those innocuous reasons why people say they watch. The cofounder of the Web site www.Television WithoutPity.com sees it in a far different way. Sara Bunting argues that viewers are not . . .

> altruistically interested in seeing whether a good match is made . . . they just want to watch these women embarrass themselves because, evidently, your only self-worth in the culture, according to this show, is if you're on television and you have a man.[2]

Ouch. Unfortunately, she may be right.

Who Am I?

I was blessed to be a pretty successful television journalist when I met Lew. I had invested my life in my career and sacrificed many nights and weekends for work when most women my age were out scouring for a husband. It felt good to have reached the goal I set for myself years before. I liked being able to say I anchored the five o'clock news in Atlanta, a top-ten television market. I had worked hard for it, sacrificed a lot, and it felt good to be successful. Did I get part of my self-worth from being a television journalist and making lots of money? You bet.

So there I was, at the top of my game—strong, independent, confident—when this man came along, and something very strange happened. As I look back on who I was after he entered the picture and I fell in love, I still cannot believe it. I was one person, and after he came into my life, I became another—a pod person whose only resemblance to the real me was the blonde hair.

I never even realized what was happening. Was it that I was so excited to finally find someone I could see myself with forever that I was more than willing to transform myself into who I thought he wanted me to be? Probably. Whatever the reason, when he said he loved me, that became my sole reason for waking up in the morning. I even projected myself into the not-too-distant future when I would have his babies, clean his house, shop for his underwear, and never look into the camera lens again. Can you believe that? All those years I gave myself to my career and had finally reached my goal, and in a nanosecond would have given it up all for the love of this man.

It was not just that Lew's love caused my love for my career to evaporate, though. It was the person I *became* as the relationship progressed that is just as weird to me now.

For example, what I considered friendly *sparring* between the two of us—that quick, witty banter that sounds like a Katharine Hepburn–Humphrey Bogart movie, which I thought was fun and showed off how we so perfectly fit mentally—was not so charming to other people. In fact, my family and friends told me after he left me that it made them uncomfortable and came off as disrespectful to me. It was not the caring conversation of two people in love but more of an exercise of one-upmanship between two competitive personalities. It took a lot of energy and brainpower to keep up with him

> I was one person, and after he came into my life, I became another—a pod person whose only resemblance to the real me was the blonde hair.

in that way, but I did it. I actually wore myself out doing it to prove to him how smart and quick-witted I was and how stimulating life with me would always be. Stimulating for him, maybe, but exhausting for me.

Here is another example of my finding self-worth solely in how I was perceived by Lew. He was an avid runner, and while I had been a tennis player and was always physically active, I was most definitely not a runner. I hate to run. Love to walk, hate to run. Three guesses what I tried with all my heart to do. I can remember one particularly humiliating Sunday when I, determined to find another thing to prove to him how worthy I was of his love, decided to go with him on a run. Let's just say I did not get far. As I walked back to his apartment and he sprinted on, I remember *knowing* in my soul that what I was doing was not right. I did not like to run and should have told him so. Instead, I felt like a failure, the girl who would never be able to keep up. I don't think I ever tried to run with him again. I'm fairly certain I would not have been invited.

The point is that a Kimberley, properly grounded in her faith, would never have tried to become something she was not. She never would have been constantly performing witty repartee when she was not up for it or trying to excel at a sport she did not like. She would have known that the person God had created her to be was perfect, just as she was, and that the *right* man for her would love her for that. Instead, she had begun to find her self-worth only in how the man she loved perceived her and the person she thought *he* wanted her to be.

What happens, then, when a woman alters herself to please a man? Even if she is being her authentic self but still sees her worth only through a man's eyes, when that man rejects her, it is a double blow. Not only has *he* left, but when he walked out the door, he took her whole validation for existence with him. That, to me, is one of the saddest repercussions of rejection: you no longer feel that you are important or significant or worth anything because he no longer does. I had that feeling in spades. But I believe that is clearly the enemy's work. (I'll talk more about this player in my story in the next chapter, but trust me; this is not someone who is on your side.) If he can get you to believe that you no longer have significance, he can also get you to believe that God must not have any plan for your life since the key to it all just left you. And nothing could be farther from the truth.

Claire

I spoke with a woman named Claire, whose own self-worth has been nearly destroyed in a heartbreaking marriage she has chosen to stay in for the sake of her four children. She tells me it is one thing to be lonely when you are single, but it is a million times worse to be lonely when you are married.

Claire feels rejected every single day. For the most part, her husband dismisses her, but when he does address her, it is in such a way as to make her feel small and stupid. He never notices when she is sick, barely says hello when he comes home from work, and at dinnertime, never compliments her cooking or has a conversation with her apart from the kids. When they do have adult alone time, any opinions she shares are discarded as uninformed and silly. There are times when she truly feels he loves the family dog more than he loves her. Claire says she *craves* some sort of affirmation even if it is just an "atta girl" and a pat on the back. She is battered beyond belief but holding on for the sake of her children, and she has lost hope that God is ever going to intervene.

What may surprise you about Claire's story is that she is a beautiful woman with a vibrant personality and lots of friends, a brilliant golfer, and a big-city television news anchor. She should be feeling pretty good about herself, don't you think?

The Plan

Over and over again God's Word tells us how very valuable we are. He knew us, knew who we would become, knew what our joys and our sorrows would be, and wrote it all down in his book even before we were born. He "knit me together in my mother's womb" (Ps. 139:13), and oh, how I love that image. Like a woman, rocking in a rocking chair, carefully, lovingly knitting a warm, beautiful sweater for someone she loves. And after we are born, God does not leave us to fend for ourselves. No, our Father promises never to leave us or forsake us and makes a special life plan for each one of us. Not just some ho-hum, average, ordinary plan either. Jesus says he came so that we could have a really great plan and *abundant* life (John 10:10). *Abundant*: "more than enough, plentiful, bountiful." Nothing ordinary about that! And if that is not enough to show any woman who feels rejected that she is more than worthy, God also tells us that he does not even want us to *worry* about anything. Not the mundane things, such as what we will eat or drink or what we will wear. And not the big things, such as what will happen tomorrow.

So here are the facts. Yes, the man you love or was hoping to love has rejected you. It is awful, and you are feeling hurt and alone. But the God who created the *universe* has not rejected you. In fact, he's crazy about you. He *chose* you before time even began. He promised never to walk out the door, and he promised that he has plans for you to have an incredible life. "'For I know the plans I have for you,' declares the Lord, 'plans to prosper you and not to harm you, plans to give you hope and a future'" (Jer. 29:11). The God of the universe! I don't know about you, but those sound like pretty good odds to me.

The truth is, while God created us to be in relationship with others, he did not intend for one person to become our whole reason for being. You see, God knows that people are fallible and will almost never live up to who we want them to be. He knows that people we love will disappoint us and that life will sometimes be disheartening. He knows relationships can be wonderful and fulfilling but also hurtful and heartbreaking. I think it breaks God's heart when our hearts are broken. And that is why he gives us mates to *complement* our lives, not to make us whole. If a man was created solely to make your life whole, then he would not be realizing the perfect plan God had for him.

> The God who created the *universe* has not rejected you. In fact, he's crazy about you.

You are loved. And you are more than worthy. It may not feel like it at this moment. You may be feeling as unloved and unworthy as a person can feel. But you are both loved and worthy. More than worthy. The One who loves you as no one else on earth ever can or ever will is there, waiting for you to know who you are to him, how important, and how very special.

Five

The Perfect Target

*The snake was a he, not an it,
and definitely not a she![1]*

—Liz Curtis Higgs

As I am writing this, the United States is engaged in the war against terrorism. It is a modern enemy unlike any we have ever faced before because there is no declared country or army for us to target. Instead, it is obscure, clandestine, unpredictable, and insidious in the fear it creates inside many of us. It threatens to attack where we are most vulnerable and when we least expect it. Exactly like Satan, the enemy I told you about earlier.

Think about my story. I got hit, unexpectedly, on the happiest weekend of my life. And that one event, those few moments inside the church, set my life in a downward spiral that nearly hijacked my faith and my very life. Rejection was Satan's ammunition. And oh, the power it had.

Little did I know then, I had actually helped him lay the groundwork for what would happen in my life. *Why?* I had deceived myself.

When Lew left me, I was so angry at God because I believed I had been a good person, a faithful churchgoer, so I thought he should have intervened to stop me from being hurt. As if those two things alone would make God so proud of me and so appreciative for what a wonderful person I had turned out to be that he would stop Lew from dumping me. Does it strike you as incongruous that not once, not one time in my entire story leading up to the altar, did this "good person" and "faithful churchgoer" ever mention discussing any of this with God? That is because I didn't. Not once. Not one single prayer.

Rejection is a lot like that infamous Southern plant kudzu. It grows out of control until it smothers everything good around it. And rejection often grows the same way until it smothers every positive thing you have ever felt about yourself. It is one of Satan's most effective, most powerful weapons in separating us from the love and the power of God at the times when we need him most.

The Deceiver

Most people today call Satan the *enemy*. I prefer the *deceiver*. That is, after all, what he's all about: deceiving us into believing that God either does not care—cannot or will not get involved—or is not even there at all during our times of greatest pain and heartbreak. Remember my state of mind in the early days after Lew left me at the altar? I did not hate Lew; I hated God. In my mind, what was the point of having a God in your life who would not or could not prevent a horrible thing from happening to you? And worship him? Forget it. There was no way I would ever step foot in a church again. This was not the kind of God to whom I wanted to bow down. He had let me down if he was even there at all. That's just how I felt.

The deceiver relished my God bashing and my mourning for Lew. He loved every miserable moment of it because he finally had me right where he wanted me—feeling isolated, hurt, angry, beaten down, and most important, hopeless. You see, if you are hopeless, it means you have lost any expectation that God is not only there with you but also at some point is going to pull you out of the mess you are in and make your life happy again. Hopelessness, complete hope- lessness, is why some people choose to end their lives when they are so low they cannot see up. And hopelessness is the exact state in which the deceiver does his best work in us. It separates us from God because it causes us to cut ourselves off from him and his power to heal us. If he can accomplish that, he has done his job.

There were certainly days when I would lie on my sofa feel- ing hopeless, thinking that life

> I did not hate Lew;
> I hated God.

today held no hope and tomorrow held no promise. I could not believe a person could have so many tears. And not once did I cry out for God to help me.

The first prayer I ever said regarding Lew was actually the last. It was soon after we met, and (on paper) he really did seem like a perfect fit. Well educated, devoted to his family, witty, funny, athletic. The problem was, in the beginning I did not feel that knee-knocking attraction. So I prayed that if this was the man he intended for me to be with, then he was going to have to help me out a little bit. Sure enough, an attraction did develop although it is pretty obvious now that it was not God's doing.

No, it was *my* doing and the deceiver's. I was not patient enough to wait on God. So my insatiable desire to be in control propelled me into a relationship that he did not intend for me. Every fiber in my intellectual being told me this was the man for me, which is exactly why my first prayer was my last. I knew that if I relinquished control and turned my relationship with Lew over to God, he might take it away. I knew what was best for me. God would see.

What God saw was disobedience. What the deceiver saw was that he had won round one. And what I ended up with was heartbreak.

It is so sad to me now to realize that all the pain could have been avoided had I just once earnestly asked God for his help, his guidance, his will to be done in my relationship with Lew. Even after Lew changed our first wedding date, despite the fact that I was disappointed, I never skipped a beat. I plowed on, prodding Lew for a new date as I continued planning the perfect wedding. Now, I'm either not all that smart or just plain stubborn because anybody with half a brain could see Lew just was not as into this wedding thing as I was. Had I consulted God and prayed for his will to be done in my life and Lew's, and for the strength to accept it on faith, I am certain my relationship would have ended, and I could have moved on with the faithful assurance that it was what was right. Sure, I would have hurt then, too, but not nearly as much, and then God and I would have been in control, not a man.

The Turning-It-Over-to-God Thing

I never consulted God. And instead I ended up with a heartbreak that
will leave a scar forever. Think of the pain we all could save ourselves
if we would just do what God tells us in the Bible to do, to trust him,
to have faith, to wait patiently. Here God has given us our very own
instruction manual for life, and we pick and choose what to believe and
what to follow.

Before I began my real walk with Christ, I just did not get the trusting
and turning-it-over-to-God thing. And I am sure a lot of women today
feel the same way. I would like to say that we have all just learned what
men have known all along: being in control is a real high. But we did not
just learn it. Think Garden of Eden. To whom did the deceiver go so
he could try to manipulate and control God? I think we all know it was
not Adam. But I do believe that women today have so embraced the
whole being-in-control thing that it has become a very effective, modern
way the deceiver has discovered to separate us from God. We think, *Hey,
I've got everything under control, so why do I need him? Thanks for the offer, God, but
I can take it from here.*

Boy, I Sure Showed Him!

Fast-forward to the present, and now, of course, I realize that it
really was not Lew but my own desire for control and my unwillingness
to surrender my will to God that got me to the altar at St. Luke's
Episcopal Church that April day. I simply was not in relationship
with God as he intended it to be, and I paid a hefty price. Not only

that, but when tragedy did strike, just as the deceiver knew, I had nothing to fall back on. I could find no comfort, no peace, even though Christ promised both. Remember, the only Bible verse I could conjure was, "My God, my God, why have you forsaken me?" (Matt. 28:46). There was simply nothing left inside of me because, in truth, there had not been much there at the start. I had been a Christian in name only, just going through the motions, and that made me a perfect target.

Let's look at the astounding number of ways I was misled, and then we'll see how God would have, had he been asked, countered the attacks. Since I never asked, the deceiver had me believing . . .

- I could control my relationship with this man and, therefore, get my way—in this case, get him to marry me.

- I knew what kind of man I needed to marry. Forget the fact that we were not, as the Bible says, *equally yoked* (2 Cor. 6:14). That would be another thing I could control once we were married.

- Warning signs are not always warning signs. Sometimes they are just roadblocks that relationships go through.

- Most men have cold feet. Changing wedding dates and not getting out of the car at the marriage license bureau will be something funny to tell the kids one day.

- God must not love me at all to make my family and me go through such a terrible ordeal.

- God could have changed the outcome either by not letting the relationship progress to the altar or by helping Lew to go through with the wedding.

- God was not there in my suffering.

- God did not hear my cries.

- Something was intrinsically wrong with me to cause a man to do such a despicable thing.

- No one else has ever been left at the altar as I was. No one has ever been so publicly humiliated. No one could possibly understand what I am going through.

- No man will ever love me again.

- I'm not worthy of a man's love.

- I will never be happy again unless a man loves me.

- I am cursed—first losing the love of my life, then my job, then my health.

- I'll never go back to church again. I won't worship God ever again.

- I will never get the "Jesus thing." Whatever it is that gives other people peace and encouragement and hope, Jesus did not give it to me.

- All those verses in the Bible that people are always quoting are just that—things somebody wrote a long time ago to make themselves feel better. They just are not true.

- I am going to be a spinster—one of those old, miserable women who lives down the street with all the cats. And I hate cats.

- I'll never feel hope in my heart again.

Amazing, isn't it? All those lies. And they surely are not unique to me. I imagine with all the broken relationships and broken promises in our society today that these lies are nearly worn out, they have been used so often. It breaks my heart that so many people are so willing, just as I was, to believe those lies—so unwilling to believe the promises of God.

God has provided a stronghold for all of us who live in Christ—a shield and a fortress against this enemy of our souls and the assault of his lies. If we remember any truth at all in our darkest hours of deepest hurt, it should be that *God loves us*. If we can remember that, it will be enough to hold us up until we can regain our equilibrium. The rest will come. He will provide what we need when we need it. Remember, he is our Father, a God who created us in his own image and loved us so much that he allowed his own Son to die a cruel and horrible death on a cross so that we could have victory over the lies and live forever with him and the truth.. All we have to do is believe it. Accept him. Trust him. Love him. And let him love us back.

Six

Protecting My Heart

Where fear is, happiness is not.

—SENECA

The strangest part of my story is that, despite everything that had happened, I missed him. I did, I missed Lew. I would look at pictures of us together and daydream about all the good times we'd had. I longed to tell him about my day, watch him practice his tee shots, talk with the waiters at our favorite Chinese restaurant, use our nicknames for each other, and for his late-night calls from the road. Lew had been my best friend for two years, and I wanted to share with him all the things I was feeling.

Family and friends begged me to be angry with him, to hate him even, and I just couldn't. I never could understand how anyone could go from one day loving someone with all your heart to the next day hating him. For me it was impossible, but oh, how I wish I could have. Had I believed he was a jerk, an idiot for not marrying me, I could have gotten over all of it a lot sooner. Being rejected by a jerk is a lot easier to overcome than being rejected by a great guy. Instead, I never hated him or felt angry at him, and not once did I think about the not-so-happy times, particularly the crummy way he left me at the altar.

The Letter

Ten days after the "altarcation," I got a FedEx letter from Lew at my mother's house. I was shaking as I opened it, fully expecting him to tell me I was a great girl, but it would never work out, that I would find someone else. To my great surprise, though, it was nothing like that. It was a beautiful letter, expressing sorrow and regret and confidence that we were meant to be together and asking what he could do to have me back. Have me back? Why? Why now? Was he feeling guilty? Well, you may want to sit down before you read this because, yes, I took him back. But it was never the same again. The hurt had been too great. There was not a day that went by that I did not feel rejected.

> In the end, he was never able to make a commitment to marriage, and in the end, I was finally able to accept it.

I have a theory that we should never second-guess our decisions because at that time we do what we think is right. I do think we can learn from bad decisions. Taking him back was a bad decision. My relationship with Lew sputtered on and off for several months after that. I did everything I could think of to get him to the altar: set a goal, work hard, never give up. My sister and closest friends never knew. Had they known, I'm certain they would have staged an intervention. In the end, he was never able to make a commitment to marriage, and in the end, I was finally able to accept it. But by that time Lew's rejection had changed me.

The Legacy of Rejection

Fear. Such a small word for such a big emotion. I have often thought someone should add more letters to the word *fear* to make it appear as gigantic on paper as it feels in real life. It has been said that hate is the opposite of love. I say it is fear. Most everything bad or scary we feel in our lives springs from it. And it is the unfortunate legacy of rejection.

I agreed to see Lew again—after he left me at the altar—out of fear. Fear of being without him. Fear of being alone. Fear that I would never find anyone to love as I had loved him. It was fear that lured me back to the man who had so hurt me. I can blame Lew for everything up until that moment at the church, for not having the guts to tell me point-blank *beforehand* that he did not want to get married. But everything after that—the months and probably years that I held on to the hope of our being together—that's all me. And what I would not give to have that time back.

Once I was able to let go and trust God, I would love to tell you my fear went away and never came back. It didn't. It simply took on other forms: in the beginning it was the fear of being rejected by someone else. After Lew, the first man I dated seriously broke it off after three months. Now, I honestly did not think this would be the man I would marry, but I did enjoy his company, and when he ended it, the feelings of rejection bubbled up into an extreme overreaction.

I cried and cried, "Not again!" even though my mind kept reminding me I would not have married him anyway. Instead, all I could think was that I had been rejected again, that no one was ever going to love me, and that I was going to be alone forever. Once again, the deceiver slithered in, wanting me to believe all the same lies he had gotten me to believe after Lew left. And he did not have to work hard. I was very willing to believe them again. The only difference this time was that I was also willing to ask God to help me disown them.

Pursuit of "The One"

Several years later, I was to discover a whole new thing to fear. And this one was just as big. I had come to the decision not to ever go on another blind date for as long as there was breath in my body. I had just come off a year of working pretty hard—okay, working *really* hard—at finding a husband. It was an exhausting, discouraging year. Nobody clicked, and, believe me, I went out with everybody anyone could find. I was practically stopping people at traffic lights, asking them if they knew anyone I could date.

Not long after my no-date declaration, a friend at church said she had someone she thought I would really like. By this time in my new walk with God, I was working at making sure I noticed when he was at work in my life, and it occurred to me this might be one of those times. Just in case he was using my *church* friend to link me up with "the one," I had better recognize the opportunity for what it was. I would hate to get to heaven and ask God why he never sent me a husband and have him say, "I did, but you wouldn't go out with him." So I agreed, albeit reluctantly, to my friend's offer of yet another blind date.

> I was practically stopping people at traffic lights, asking them if they knew anyone I could date.

Bingo. Finally, a good one! My friend was right. This man was tall and handsome, smart and funny, and so easy to talk to. We hit it off immediately, like people with good chemistry always do, and ended up dating for a while. And I remember the moment I first realized that I just might be able to love someone again the way I loved Lew. I was standing in my shower, getting ready for a date, with all the high-school excitement you have when a relationship's new, and I started crying, crying so hard I could not stop. The fear had totally consumed me—fear so overpowering that it nearly paralyzed me. I got out of the shower and almost canceled the date. *Why not cancel it,* I thought, *and end the relationship now? It will never work out in the end anyway. And I cannot let myself fall in love again only to have my heart broken by another man. Best to end it now. Protect my heart.*

God heard my cries and fear, and I did not cancel my date that evening. I ended up dating that man for months after that. The relationship ultimately did come to an end for very good reasons on his part, and while I was sad, I never once felt *rejected*.

Rejecting Rejection

Imagine what a victory that was. How far I had come! Years before, I was broken and hopeless, unwilling to trust the truth God had offered me. But I had become whole and hopeful, and this time I was the one doing the rejecting: rejecting the lies the deceiver wanted me to believe.

> "You're alone. You'll always be alone," he whispers in my ear.

I have come to the conclusion that there are three players driving us in the events of our lives: us (our own self-will), the deceiver, and God. In every single event, good or bad, the deceiver will fight for control of the wheel. As we deepen our walks with God, we *must* learn to recognize when the deceiver is at work. He tried but failed to squash my hope of ever finding a husband by making me afraid I would never love anyone but Lew. He tried but failed to make me believe that no relationship will ever work out. He continues to try, and he continues to fail, to make me believe that I will never love or be loved again. The good news, the victorious news, is that God did that. God and his patient love for me.

Slowly, slowly I learned to trust God and to reject the deceiver's lies. But the first step was *recognizing* those lies for what they were. Just as I now can see when God is at work in my life, I can see just as clearly when the deceiver is at work. For example, sometimes on Friday afternoons, when the "coupled world" begins its weekends, I can feel him winding up: "You're alone. You'll always be alone," he whispers in my ear.

Not only do I recognize that for what it is, but I can now counter it with God's truth: I am never *alone.* God is always with me, and he has blessed me with a wonderful family and precious friends, and *one day* I will be one of those couples making plans for their weekend.

How do I know that? Because I know God. I have seen him work in my life, firsthand, up close and personal. I know he keeps his promises. And I know that until he fulfills that promise, he knows I'm way too weak to combat the deceiver on my own. He is too relentless, and I would never have the strength. But when God infuses me with his Spirit, I can withstand the deceiver's never-ending barrage. God never fails to deliver on his promise to give me strength when I am weary and power when I am weak. Never.

Remember that. Perfect love, God's unfailing love, drives out the deceiver, and along with him, it drives out *fear*.

Seven

Man's Rejection, God's Protection

As long as you don't forgive,
who and whatever it is will occupy
rent-free space in your mind.[1]

—ISABELLE HOLLAND

Nobody knows better than me that when you have been rejected and nearly mortally wounded by someone you love, the last thing you want to do is forgive that person. Plenty of other things come to mind you would like to do to him or her, but forgiveness is not one of them. At least, at the beginning. But forgiving him or her and forgiving *yourself* are essential steps, not just in healing from rejection but in getting your relationship with God where it truly needs to be. Forgiveness is a biggie.

For me, forgiving Lew did not come for a long time. That's because at first, I didn't blame Lew for leaving me as much as I blamed myself and God. I blamed God for pretty much everything: for not forcing me to see the relationship as it was, for not encouraging Lew to end things before they got to the altar, for not stepping in and *making* Lew marry me—you name it, and in my mind it was God's fault.

When it was not God's fault, it was mine. What did I do to cause a man to leave me at the altar? There must have been something terribly lacking in me, something abhorrent about me that so turned him off he could not bear the thought of spending his life with me. What had I failed to develop in my character or personality or abilities that forced him away? Or perhaps I had done something to make God angry with me, so angry that he allowed this terrible thing to happen. Was God trying to teach me something or punish me for something I was not doing or something I had done? Surely this had all been my fault. It is so strange to me now that I never put any of the blame on Lew until much later. And even then it was not really blame. It was just a more adult, mature understanding of things, a more Godlike understanding of things.

> Yes, a man had rejected me, but God was still there protecting me and loving me and trying to draw me close to him if I would just let him.

Not long after I got left at the altar, God planted a thought deep in my soul from a stranger who stopped me in the mall. It has now become my mantra anytime I feel rejected in any area of my life, not just in those of the heart.

She said, "Kimberley, I heard what happened to you, and I'm so sorry. But I have just one thing to say: man's rejection, God's protection."

And with that she walked away, leaving me to ponder for a long time that short but powerful statement. Yes, a man had rejected me, but God was still there protecting me and loving me and trying to draw me close to him if I would just let him. He wanted to prepare me for a brand-new relationship . . . with him. Back then, I was not ready for a new relationship. I still wanted to hang on to the old one. I wanted to be in charge.

Who's in Control?

I held on tightly to my desire for control. Even on those miserable days on my sofa, when it felt as if my life would never be good again, I refused to give it up. Just like a screaming child holding on to a toy she does not want to turn over, I could not give God control of my life. Deep down I knew that it was the one thing God wanted from me, the one thing he was waiting for before my healing could begin. But in the beginning I just could not do it. *Why?* If I am honest, I would have to say that I was worried that what I wanted for my life and what God wanted for my life might not be the same thing. And I was unable to trust that God's plan was better.

I do not remember the exact moment God helped me snap out of my sadness, but I do know that when I was finally able to slowly relinquish control was when I started healing. Maybe I was just exhausted from trying to go it alone. Maybe I just decided to stop being stubborn. Whatever the root cause of my long-overdue obedience, God and I were able to work it out together over time.

One thing that helped me was something a close friend once told me she did with problems—a mental exercise, if you will. I would start each day picturing God sitting on his throne and my standing before him with my control in my hands, wrapped up like a package, handing it to him, like a gift. I would also ask him to take away my *desire* for control and to help me let it go. Day after day I did that, and can you guess what happened? To my great surprise, rather than feeling as if I was losing a cherished friend, I actually felt as if a giant load was being lifted from me. Being in control may have felt like a high, but in truth it was a heavy burden. And once I could give it to God and learn to *trust* in him, a quiet peace settled over me like snow drifting down on an early winter's morning.

Jeremiah 17:7–8 says this:

> Blessed is the [woman] who trusts me, God,
>> the woman who sticks with God.
> They're like trees replanted in Eden,
>> putting down roots near the rivers—
> Never a worry through the hottest of summers,
>> never a dropping leaf,
> of droughts serene and calm through
>> bearing fresh fruit in every season (MSG)

I love that scripture because it makes me think of the beautiful mimosa trees that grew by the lake on the ranch where I grew up—so strong and so *peaceful*, gently swaying in the refreshing breeze. That is exactly how I felt when I learned to trust in him.

I hear stories all the time of women trying to manipulate circumstances to get men to do what they want them to do. One woman I know moved her entire life, away from her family and friends and successful career, to another city to be with the man she loved when he relocated with his job. She had no promise of an engagement ring, and she never received one. She had assumed by uprooting herself for him, she could manipulate him into marrying her. Instead, she eventually moved back home, feeling totally rejected and embarrassed.

I don't want to be too hard on these women because I know better than anybody that a good man is hard to find, and sometimes you do feel as if you need to do whatever it takes to land him. But manipulation is nothing more than trying to get a desired effect by controlling someone else, and in the end, it never works. Both people in a relationship have to come to it willingly and happily.

I finally learned that, if I feel I must manipulate and plan and conspire to get what I want, then it is probably not God's will for me. Rather than walking away after Lew canceled our first wedding date, I just set another one, and frankly, I did not feel victorious even though I got what I wanted. Manipulating, controlling, I can just imagine God on his throne, shaking his head at my willful, misguided determination.

The other half of the giving-up-control equation was learning to wait patiently on God. That, for me, was as hard as anything I have ever had to do. Patience is a virtue, but it is one with which I was not blessed, although I am trying to learn it. A friend

> I finally learned that, if I feel I must manipulate and plan and conspire to get what I want, then it is probably not God's will for me.

of mine heard me say this, and she laughed, saying, "One thing you never want to do, Kimberley, is to *pray* for patience because God may just respond by giving you trials and problems through which to learn it. Remember, God does answer prayer; so be careful what you ask him to give you."

I also work in a field that is the antithesis of patience. People in television news are trained to meet daily deadlines. Reporters have to submit their news pieces by a certain time in order to get them in the newscast, no excuses. You also get used to instant results. You go shoot a story, and it airs that day. No waiting months for a project to be done as most people in the business world have to do. So I had a double whammy when it came to waiting patiently because I was wired and trained to do just the opposite. I wanted things when I wanted them, which is not how God works.

Control and Patience

I am grateful for a Bible full of flawed people like me, in this case control freaks—strong-willed, "stiffnecked" people, who thought they could manage just fine on their own, without God's help, thank you very much. And you don't have to read much further than the very first book, Genesis, to find the CEO of Control. She was Sarah Abram's wife. Sarai makes me look like an amateur.

The God of the universe had told Abram that he would become the father of so many heirs that there are not even enough stars in the sky to count them all. So Sarai took it upon herself to make it happen. Granted, I can see her concern. Abram was in his eighties, and she was in her seventies. Still, the *God of the universe* told them it would be so. You would think she could trust that. Instead, Sarah had to help God keep his promise (read: control the situation) by having a servant named Hagar sleep with Abram to give him an heir. Several years later, still not trusting God to keep his promise, Sarah even laughed at the Lord when she overheard him telling Abraham that she would become pregnant with a son at age ninety. Sarah probably wished she had not laughed because sure enough, she did get pregnant. God kept his promise, accomplishing his purpose despite her lack of faith and attempt at self-reliance.

I had a lot of work to do once my new walk with God began. Those two big things, letting go of control and waiting patiently for God to work, did not come easily. They took, still take, daily prayer and practice. And if I said I was completely healed, I would not be telling the truth. There are still many occasions when I revert into my old pattern of wanting to take control. The difference now is that I often recognize when I am doing it and can usually put the brakes on before I mess things up, thank goodness. It is surprisingly liberating to let someone else have the wheel for a change. But the most amazing thing I have discovered is that the closer I get to God, the more *my* will becomes *his* will. The two don't fight as much for prominence in my mind anymore; more and more they become the same.

I'll leave you with one final thought about control and what it really says about us and our faith when we fail to turn control of our lives over to God. It's a funny line, courtesy of one of my pastors at church:

You know the only difference between you and God?
God doesn't think he's you!

Truth or Fairy Tale?

And now, back to forgiveness. As the weeks and months went by, God also showed me that I needed to forgive myself and be forgiven, but the reasons are not what I mentioned above. I needed to come to terms with the fact that I had been controlling, that I had not put my trust in God, and that I had played a huge part in being left at the altar. I had to step up to the plate and face the person I was. For me, it was critical to my healing that I take responsibility for my own hardheadedness and my shallow faith. Once I was able to do that, I could look back on the relationship as it *really was*, not the fairy tale I had chosen to recall. I could finally deal with the truth, aspects of our relationship that might have, check that, *would* have become major problems down the road.

For example, I remember convincing myself that he would go to church with me every Sunday *once we got married*. Now, I like to think that I am a pretty smart girl, but that was not smart to assume a grown man would suddenly change a lifelong pattern of *not going* to church every week just because he was now married to me. No doubt about it, that would have become a huge issue in our marriage, leading to countless fights when Sunday mornings rolled around, and I would have had to go to

> I had played a huge part in being left at the altar.

church alone. How could that not have been a red flag to me? The Bible says we should not be yoked together with unbelievers (2 Cor. 2:14). I knew that. I ignored it.

Today, I cannot imagine it. Because if it is not important to your mate to worship God regularly, how can he think it is important for your children to go to church either? Man's rejection, God's protection. I spent a lot of time on my knees on this one. And as I began to truly reflect on our relationship, I could see many things I had chosen to ignore that would have, no doubt, led to heartbreak, disappointment, and probably divorce. God and his amazing grace helped me finally to see that, yes, I needed to forgive myself and I needed God to forgive me, not because I had done something to cause Lew to leave me, but because I had not been the person God intended me to be, and that was a woman after God's own heart. I was after Lew's heart, not God's.

Remember Claire, the woman who feels rejected in her marriage? Claire admits that there were warning signs about Robert's character, which she ignored while they were dating, long before they lived together as husband and wife. He was not a godly man. In fact the only time they went to a church together was when they went through mandatory pastoral counseling before their wedding. He never particularly valued her opinion on anything, never treasured her as someone special. But he did love *dating* her. That is because she was fun and fun-loving and enjoyed partying and being with other people as much as he did.

But looking back Claire says there was one thing that had given her pause. She remembers feeling a lot of discomfort when they would go to restaurants, and Robert would be rude to the waiters and waitresses, as if they were nobodies and unimportant. Claire knew deep down that his actions said something about Robert's character and his lack of care and concern for other people. She would later discover that often also extended to her. Still, she shrugged it off.

What is most strange about Claire's predicament is that she knew better. She had been brought up in a godly home where going to church mattered, where kindness to others, including strangers, was expected, where the opinion of each family member was important and valued.

Claire married Robert anyway. Like me, she was after *his* heart, not God's. Unfortunately for her, she is still suffering the results.

Facing Forgiveness

Now to forgiving Lew. Once I was finally able to see things from God's perfect perspective, I knew Lew had been wrong in how he rejected me. I could never fault anyone for stopping a marriage that he or she did not want, no matter when the decision was made. But what I needed to forgive Lew for was that deep down, at that time, he simply did not want to get married, either to me or to anyone else (it doesn't matter which), and he never hinted that might be the case.

Yes, I had been controlling, but Lew was a grown man who made decisions every day as the owner of his company. Not being able to come to me, his future wife, about the biggest personal decisions in his life, look me in the eye and say, "Kimberley, I love you; I love

> There was plenty of blame to go around, and I needed to forgive us both.

being with you, but I just don't want to get married," was not fair or right. Period. "I do not want to be married." Of course, I would have been upset, I would have cried, there would certainly have been a scene, and that would have been uncomfortable for him, but it would have been the noble thing to do, the right thing to do. It would have spared me the very deep wound of rejection that he inflicted by doing it at the altar just hours before our wedding. By then my expectations were so high, and my mind was already so deeply entrenched in our future together that the jolt nearly immobilized me.

Unfortunately, though, that is what happened. And I had to forgive him for whatever it was that had kept him from ending things sooner. I needed to remember that he is human just as I am. There was plenty of blame to go around, and I needed to forgive us both.

Crossing the Bridge

God talks a lot about forgiveness in the Bible. It is one of the cornerstones of faith. Without bestowing it on others, we become bitter and resentful. Without receiving it ourselves, we become mired in guilt. Either one on its own is bad; both at the same time is excruciating. Neither one allows us to have the amazing life (the Bible actually calls it "abundant" life, and no, that does not mean he wants us all to be *rich*) God wants for us. And God so wants us to have an incredible life.

That is why, I believe, it grieved him so much when Adam and Eve introduced sin into the world because it separated us from him and prevented us from experiencing life in the wonderful way he intended. Sin just messed everything up because it caused us to hurt and betray and be angry at one another. But that is where Jesus came in. In the beginning of time, God established a law that basically said that man could make things right with him by offering a blood sacrifice. Back then that meant sacrificing an animal that was perfect. When Jesus, the only person who was ever perfect and never sinned, came and died on the cross, *he* became the blood substitute. All God asks us to do is to believe that and accept him into our hearts. When we do that, we are forgiven. In Ephesians 1:7 Paul says, "In him we have redemption through his blood, the forgiveness of sins." It is an awesome plan for us if you think about it because God is just giving us a free gift that we could not possibly earn. That is why it is called *grace*. Pretty amazing grace if you ask me.

I tell you all of that to show you that forgiveness is a big one with God. Otherwise, why would he allow his own Son to die so we could have it? God forgives me for everything, including deliberately and willfully choosing not to trust him with my life. And in turn he calls on me to grant that same grace, the same forgiveness, to Lew. "Forgive as the Lord forgave you" (Col. 3:13).

The really neat thing about God is that, not only does he forgive, but he also *forgets*. He does not constantly remind us of how bad we have been. It is critical to healing that we stop beating ourselves up over it and let it go, just as God has. Once I took responsibility for my disobedience, there were many times I was angry and disappointed with myself, wishing like crazy that I had not made such a mess of things. The deceiver loved it when I traveled to that place because, when I did, I separated myself from God's truth. In him we are forgiven. It is forgotten, over, done. He does not want us to live always dredging up in our minds the pain of how we have messed things up or how others have hurt us. That, my dear, is not abundant life.

On a Roll!

Once you finally get the hang of this forgiveness thing, it feels so good to free yourself from the hurt that you want to do it again and again. Hopefully, there aren't that many people in your life who need such forgiveness or from whom you need forgiveness, but if there are, I suggest while you are on a roll, do it! I think I had gotten myself to such a place and was really beginning to feel as if my new relationship with God was shaping up that I knew there was one other thing God wanted, God required, me to do. Forgive my dad.

I reflected a lot on Dad after Lew left. I guess the feelings of abandonment from Lew dredged up the same feelings of abandonment from my dad, feelings that I had not had time to dwell on when I was younger. I remember a strange and eerie dream I had one night not long after being left at the altar. I dreamed I had come home late from work and found Lew asleep on the sofa, the TV showing snow (as it used to in the old days late at night) as if Lew had fallen asleep watching me anchoring the news. I leaned down to kiss him on the head, but when he opened his eyes, it was not Lew; it was my dad.

Now, I only had a couple of psychology classes in college, but it seemed pretty clear to me that the two situations were wrapped tightly together in my brain. It was finally time to grieve my dad's leaving and to forgive him too. And so, seventeen years after he left my mom, I called my dad and met with him and did it face-to-face. I don't think I said out loud, "I forgive you," but I think he felt the spirit of my forgiveness as we were sitting together and talking after all that time. And I knew it in my heart. It felt really good to finally be obedient to God and to let go of the hurt of that rejection as well. But I have to admit that had Lew not rejected me as he did, had I not been forced to face a lot of things about myself, I am not certain I ever would have gotten to a place where I wanted to or could have forgiven my dad.

Free at Last

Man's rejection, God's protection. Yes, Lew had rejected me, but God was protecting me in so many ways. He had allowed Lew's rejection to free me from a lifetime of an unforgiving spirit. I think I also learned that life is not always black or white. There is a lot of gray. People are not always good or bad. In fact, rarely are they one or the other. Good people can sometimes do bad things. They are flawed, and they make mistakes, sometimes for reasons they believe to be valid. We must be willing to accept people's frailties, their humanness, and to forgive them when they hurt us . . . just as God forgives us.

Eight

Left at the Altar Too

We know what we are,
but know not what we may be.

—SHAKESPEARE, *HAMLET*

Going back to work a few weeks after my wedding disaster was something I had not been looking forward to, to say the least. I would have much rather stayed holed up in my bedroom, feeling sorry for myself, but there was the tiny matter of the mortgage that had to be paid.

The last time I had seen my coworkers was when I had happily, blissfully waved good-bye my last day of work before my wedding. So I dreaded all the sad looks I knew I was going to get and wondered how many times I would have to be hugged and pitied as I recounted the horrible event. Not only that, I would have to appear *on television* and smile and pretend to be perky! (I actually learned that getting back into your regular routine is a great salve. It's like learning to type: if you keep hitting the keys long enough, soon you do it automatically, and that held true on the anchor desk. One day I realized I wasn't *pretending* to be perky anymore. I really felt perky again.)

I immediately felt guilty that I had dreaded going back because my coworkers lovingly held me up those first few weeks back. And it was not just them. I came to realize pretty quickly that a lot of people in this world have been rejected. And many of those people, men and women, were kind enough to write cards and letters to tell me they understood. Most were from women whose husbands had left them with children to raise on their own. I could see that their loads were so much greater than mine. I had only myself to think about. All of those women had dealt with their hurt and pain while also continuing to meet the needs of their families. They were inspiring. And so *hopeful*. These women had not just experienced rejection as I had; they had come out victorious on the other side. I'd like to share a few of their stories with you:

One of my sorority sisters and I went through the same thing you are going through. My friend had *three* wedding invites printed up. Now we both have great husbands and have been married a long time.

Thirty years ago my fiancé called off our huge society wedding two weeks before. Six years later, when he came back, I had evolved to the point where I wasn't interested at all.

I was divorced after a twenty-five year marriage. But I just stayed close to God and trusted him. I raised my son, and eight years later, the Lord gave me a wonderful Christian husband.

I had a similar experience thirty years ago. It was painful, of course, but as a result, it enabled me to enjoy several careers, including one as a nurse and another as a teacher. A twenty-five year marriage later to a wonderful man allowed me the opportunity to earn a master's degree. Now I have three great children and a darling grandson.

I met a wonderful man; we fell deeply in love and became engaged. He resided in Cleveland, and I lived in Atlanta. I resigned my job of fourteen years to relocate to Cleveland to be with him. After a couple of months, I noticed a drastic change in his behavior . . . I tried to get him to open up, but finally I decided to move back to Atlanta. It wasn't until two years later I found out why he reacted the way he did after I relocated to his hometown . . . where he resided with his legally married wife and children. I'm happy to say I'm really okay now. In December of that very same year, I adopted a baby boy, and today he is three years old. He has been and is a real joy to my life.

I've experienced the same thing, and I came out on top with a great guy. We've been married forty years. There are thousands of men who would give you the world if they had a chance, even my husband, but he's too old.

While all those letters warmed my heart and made me smile, still I was sad. And frankly, while life seemed to have worked out okay for them, I had no illusion that it ever would for me. When you are as low as I was, you can't imagine ever smiling again, let alone laughing. Your whole reason for living had just evaporated, or so you think.

For me, doing the everyday things that used to make me happy just didn't anymore. My daily exercise at the park ended in tears every time I saw a woman with a stroller. Seeing moms and dads with their kids at church made me cry. Couples at restaurants choked me up. My pain nearly paralyzed me. I even turned away the very people who wanted to help me. I rarely answered the phone and even

> Other people had been left at the altar, too, even if not in exactly the same way I had.

admitted to one close friend who had come to town to take me to dinner that I had been dreading her visit because I didn't want to hear about how great her life was. I just didn't want to hear about anyone's husband, children, or great vacation, since it now appeared I would never experience any of the above.

Fortunately my friends ignored my bad behavior, and I found out I was not alone. Other people had been left at the altar, too, even if not in exactly the same way I had. And their pain and grief were as real and deep as mine.

Around the Lunch Table

Sit around any lunch table with a group of women, and chances are somebody there is in the throes of rejection. Either she has just been dumped or served divorce papers, not gotten a call back from a date she really liked, or is dying of loneliness from being single or from being married. And if not one of those girls around the table, one of them knows someone who is. In fact, I could put a name to each one of those scenarios just from my own circle of friends.

If you listen to these stories long enough, you will discover that, while every woman feels her story is completely unique and no one in the world could possibly understand what she is going through, the truth is that nobody's story is ever truly unique. No matter what the circumstances or whether you are rich or poor, young or old, a rocket scientist or a high-school dropout, and no matter what part of the world you come from, every single one of us is enduring or has endured the same pitiful feelings of being rejected: the same pain, hurt, disappointment, loss of self-worth, and hopelessness. *The very same things.*

But what is great about the stories I am about to share is that out of that hopelessness grew the most amazing things. All of them went on to have these wonderfully full and incredible lives because they refused to let their rejection define who they would become. They had to fight; don't get me wrong. Theirs are some dramatic stories that took them to some very sad places. But as you read, see if you can detect the common thread that makes them so much alike, besides the fact that these are some pretty gutsy women.

Billie

Billie was a child of the fifties—a cute, perky blonde whose adult life began as millions of other women in her generation. After a brief stint as a flight attendant (or *stewardess* as they were called then, and just to add to the visual, that was when all stewardesses had to be under thirty and weigh about as much as a suitcase), she married an attractive, preppy salesman she met through her roommate.

It was not long before Billie and Ralph married, and not long after that they were the parents of four young children. But despite outward appearances, this was not a happy household. It was during those early years that Ralph began making Billie feel small. At first it was in minor ways, such as complaining about a meat loaf that he thought wasn't good or a bathroom sink that he thought wasn't clean.

But as the years went on, Ralph's rejection of Billie grew mean. He said things such as, "I'm stuck with you forever because no one else would want you," or "It's wives like you who cause men to have affairs." Nice. Billie says Ralph beat her down so much year after year that she eventually lost herself. That cute, perky, blonde flight attendant had become someone she despised.

She stayed in the marriage for several reasons: first, people back then just did not get divorced, plus she would not have wanted that for her children anyway, but mostly she still loved Ralph and was willing to wait and work for any crumb of compassion he might hand out. Perhaps, she thought, if her dinners were a little tastier, the kids were a little cleaner, she was a little prettier, or if she worked a little harder, he would love her.

But after twelve years of all that wedded bliss, Ralph finally walked out. And wait till you hear how it happened.

Billie and the kids, now ages six to twelve, had decorated the station wagon with a banner that read "Welcome Home, Daddy!" and made a surprise trip to the airport to pick him up from a business trip. That was when you could actually go all the way to the gates. As Ralph got off the plane and saw his family waiting for him, he started fumbling to find his wedding ring, which was buried in his pocket, and put it back on its rightful finger. *Busted!* Right there in the airport terminal in front of his wife and children.

On the drive home, Billie finally had to face what she somehow never suspected: her husband was having an affair. Oh, if it had been only *an* affair. When they got home, when Ralph wasn't looking, Billie began going through his belongings. Somehow she remembered the combination to his briefcase and opened it. Inside were literally *hundreds* of women's phone numbers on cards, pieces of paper, and cocktail napkins. When she confronted Ralph, Billie said, rather than scrambling for excuses and denying it, he seemed relieved that he finally had gotten caught. That night he asked for a divorce.

After an excruciatingly painful night, Billie woke up the next morning, and a calm had settled over her. She then knew for sure what Ralph had been telling her all along: she did not belong on earth. She had obviously been a bad wife and probably a bad mother—so bad, in fact, that her children would be better off without her. She was worthless and out of hope. And so, that day Billie swallowed three dozen sleeping pills and hid the bottle so no one would find it before she could die.

Three days later, Billie woke up in the hospital with her pastor leaning over her bed. She told him she had dreamed that she had been in hell and asked him if that is, in fact, where she would now go.

Billie spent the next two weeks in a mental health facility where she realized that there are people in the world in far worse situations than hers. She spent a great deal of time thanking God that she was not successful in her suicide attempt and promising him that, if he would give her another chance, she would make something of her life and be the mother her children so needed. She would prove Ralph wrong.

Billie got her wish from God. He gave her more than enough strength to move forward, along with a loving family and faithful friends who were there to help. She got a job at a savings and loan as a switchboard operator, and instead of seeing it as the dead-end job it was, Billie embraced it, anointing herself "the chairman of the board." She took pride in her ability to bring home a paycheck, took in boarders to pay the bills, began to dress like the executives she saw coming in every day, and would later move up the ladder at that savings and loan. It took time, but Billie was finally able to see herself, not as rejected and discarded, but as someone worthy and wonderful.

Fast-forward twenty-one years. Billie's children are grown and out on their own. She had dated through the years but not seriously and decided it was time to get serious about finding someone new to love. She joined a video dating service, and it was not long before she met Doug. They married eight months later. That was twelve years ago, and today Billie and Doug are blissfully, happily married, like two teenagers in love.

> No matter how dark it is for you now, God will put the sun in the sky tomorrow, and if not tomorrow, the day after that.

Billie also made good on her promise to God to pay forward his grace and goodness to others. Once a week she and her dog Mattie visit children at her local children's hospital, giving the boys and girls a reason to smile and someone furry to tell their secrets to.

What does Billie want you to know? First and foremost, God gave her a second chance to know that she was loved. He wanted her to know that he loved her, whether any man ever did again or not. And God did not just give her a second chance but the courage and strength to move on through her pain.

Second, she wants you to know that no matter how dark it is for you now, God will put the sun in the sky tomorrow, and if not tomorrow, the day after that.

Third, she wants you to know that being happy is often a *choice*. She *chose* to live her life, the life that God intended. She chose survival. She chose joy.

Has she finally shed all those ugly feelings of rejection? Not all. Even today, Billie says, Doug can say something innocuous that will trigger the fears of so long ago: *Is he going to reject me too? Is he going to divorce me?* But she knows in her heart that he is not.

Elizabeth

It has been said that the things that initially attract us to someone are the things, in the end, that will drive us crazy. You are attracted to him because he is successful, but then you become angry when he spends too much time at work. You think it is cute that he is the life of the party, but then you get embarrassed when he drinks too much. You like the fact that he is handsome, but then you get peeved when he thinks so too.

Elizabeth learned that the hard way. She and Ernie had not been married forty-eight hours before she began experiencing feelings of rejection. Not physically, because everything was fine in that department, but much like Billie's husband had behaved, Ernie began criticizing and dismissing Elizabeth on their honeymoon. One of her strongest memories of what should have been a glorious week in Antigua was when they were out sightseeing in the village. If Elizabeth fell behind a few steps or walked ahead to look in a shop window, for some reason, that irritated Ernie. It was as if he was determined to control her, even the way she walked down the street.

Not a comforting way to begin a life together.

Ernie was a prominent surgeon in a medium-sized city, a well-respected member of his church and the community. Elizabeth was his equally respected wife, who devoted herself to her husband, her children, and her faith. For her, divorce was never an option, which makes you sad for her when you hear how unhappy and lonely her married life became.

Those things that initially attracted Elizabeth to Ernie did, indeed, become the very things that eventually tore them apart. The fact that he was a stable, well-established doctor was attractive in the beginning. And yes, she had to learn to live with the fact that he worked long hours away from home and spent much of his time at home decompressing from all that work. It was not perfect, but if that had been all there was to it, Elizabeth could have lived with that.

As the years went on, though, the other character attributes Elizabeth had put in Ernie's "positive" column when they were dating bizarrely turned into "negatives." For example, Ernie had a profound sense of integrity, but it caused him to become irritated with Elizabeth's dramatic way of telling stories: she did not just get caught in traffic; she was *in the car all day!*

Ernie had a brilliant mind, but he always managed to find a way to remind Elizabeth about how much smarter he was than her. Ernie had a quiet, restrained, composed demeanor, which served him well as a surgeon, but the way Elizabeth talked too much and laughed too loudly annoyed him. Eventually, Elizabeth began to feel that Ernie was disgusted with her.

Perhaps it was the stress of his work, perhaps something deeper, but Ernie also became a very angry man, at least when he was at home. Even discovering a tiny Sweet 'N Low package on the table or finding Elizabeth on the phone when he got home would set him off. The world never knew what was going on inside this seemingly perfect household, but for Elizabeth it was bordering on mental and emotional torture.

Because she was a woman of profound faith, Elizabeth turned to the one place she knew she could find the answer: God. Prayer eventually led her to a well-known Christian counselor (Ernie had refused to go to couple's counseling, saying *she* was the one with the problem), who gave her an answer all right. But it was one that Elizabeth was not so sure she could accomplish.

The counselor told Elizabeth to respond to Ernie's anger with *blessing.* Can you imagine the look on her face when he told her that? How in the world was she supposed to do that? She was a strong person, a "naturally buoyant person," she likes to say, and she wanted to be obedient to God, but that was asking a lot. Still, she did it. She began responding to Ernie's anger with blessing.

First, at her counselor's advice, Elizabeth made a list of all the positive aspects of his character she knew were still there, the ones she could still love and respect: he was a man of God and of prayer, the glimpses of his integrity, his ability to provide for his family, his kindness to their children.

She prayed for him. Not just alone, but with close friends who would sit on the floor and pray out loud the prayers in Stormie Omartian's book *The Power of a Praying Wife.*

She made Ernie a priority. Rather than being on the phone with a girlfriend when he arrived home, she greeted him at the door, hugged him, looked him in the eyes, and showed him she cared about his day. Elizabeth clothed herself in compassion, whether it was returned to her or not.

The good thing is that one day it was returned. Elizabeth saw Ernie's car pull in the driveway, and normally she would have hung up the phone so as not to upset him, but this time it was an important call with a friend who needed her. When he came in and saw her, he cut his eyes at her and stormed off to their bedroom. When she finally hung up the phone, fully aware of the wrath she was about to incur, Elizabeth raised her hands and gave Ernie to God, saying, "Lord, I give you Ernie. I give you his anger."

She then followed him into the bedroom and poured herself out to him. Rather than being defensive and trying to explain why she was on the phone, she told him over and over how thankful she was for him, how much she loved and respected him. Elizabeth says what happened next was nothing short of God's miracle. Ernie's entire physique softened. Right there in the bedroom, his whole demeanor made a complete 180-degree turn. At that moment, after three months of prayer and affirmation and tenderness, Elizabeth says the dance finally changed. Ernie never yelled at or became irritated with her again. That was three months before he died unexpectedly at the age of fifty-one.

Elizabeth still reflects on those years of feeling rejected, of not being valued by her husband, and the pain and hurt she lived with every day. But thankfully her memories do not end there. She prefers to dwell on the happy three months they shared before he died, with Ernie feeling loved and respected and Elizabeth finally feeling *treasured*.

Kristen

Kristen's is the kind of story Hollywood makes into movies:

The players: a beautiful young woman and her husband, a professional athlete.

The setting: a small city and then the "big time."

The premise: the rise of a glamorous career and the dramatic, jaw-dropping fall of a marriage.

The ending: Wait until you hear.

Kristen met Mike as she finished her final year in college in a not-so-big city where he was starting his professional athletic career with a not-so-big team. But he was paying his dues, he was talented, and everyone knew he would not be there long. Kristen and Mike soon married, and despite the fact that the young couple did not have much to live on except love, Kristen says those were the happiest years of their life together. Who needed real curtains when you had perfectly good sheets?

Sure enough, Mike made his move, but it was a disappointing start to his life in the big time. Injuries plagued him, and there were times when his athletic future was uncertain. It was during those times that

Kristen says Mike began to change. She knew the uncertainty he was facing was hard on him, so when he began to disappear with no explanation, she never suspected it was anything serious, just his working out frustration. Even when she found cigarette wrappers in their car, she dismissed it, despite the fact that neither she nor Mike smoked.

During this time, Kristen immersed herself in the community, serving on charity boards, helping to raise money for worthy causes, making speeches—things that were helping to solidify *Mike's* place in the hearts and minds of their new city. She would help raise lots of money for a charity event, and it would be *his* name that appeared in the paper. In public, everyone wanted to talk about him, never about her. Her only worth was in being Mike's wife, it seemed. She lived in his shadow, but that was okay. To Kristen, *they* were the team.

Within two years, fame hit. Mike's career was back on track, and he was fast becoming a star. Fans loved him. Little boys nationwide had his poster on their bedroom walls. Kristen and Mike became the *it* couple. Everyone wanted them at their event, party, or bar mitzvah. He was the hero, and she was his beautiful, charming wife. It all looked so perfect.

Soon, though, Mike began disengaging from Kristen. At first he would discourage her from traveling with the team to certain cities. When he was home, he would find excuses not to go to family functions. But Mike's rejection of Kristen eventually escalated into bullying and increasingly hostile physical and emotional abuse. That sweet, innocent boy who had just wanted to play ball was becoming a man bubbling over with arrogance and pride.

Kristen says in those years, she put blinders on. She lost touch with reality, preferring not to pay attention to the rejection she was feeling deep down. She tried practicing what she thought was forgiveness by turning the other cheek. She dug into her faith, joining Bible studies, believing that if she was a "good enough" Christian, God would protect her and her marriage.

However, Kristen could not ignore the call that came in the middle of one night when Mike was on the road with the team. It was from someone who had proof that he was having an affair. Finally, words to match her buried fear. Kristen says it was as if the bottom dropped out of her soul. Even as she told herself it wasn't true (after all, people make up stuff about famous people all the time), she called him and confronted him immediately. He, of course, denied it. And although she desperately wanted to believe him, Kristen stopped eating and sleeping.

Mike finally admitted to the affair four months later. But Kristen says that was only because she had gathered so much evidence against him that he could no longer deny it—cell phone records, credit card statements, other people's accounts of seeing him with other women. That day Mike admitted to having five affairs. (He told her after their divorce was final that there had actually been *hundreds*.)

By the time of his confession, Mike had become internationally famous, and his affairs were public information. But fame had so twisted things that, rather than feeling sympathy from fans, Kristen was the one who felt isolated and alone. As his star continued to rise, she hit bottom, rarely leaving her house for fear of hearing more stories of her husband's infidelity. It was as if the whole world had rejected her and was relishing in her heartbreak.

Kristen says she tried everything from couple's therapy to Christian intervention, but Mike was unable to stop being unfaithful, and she finally reached her breaking point. She asked him to move out, although she admits she was secretly hoping that would motivate Mike to get professional help so that they could rebuild their marriage. Unfortunately, Mike's idea of getting help was moving in with "the other woman." He filed divorce papers within months.

> She found her purpose in helping others, not just with her professional training but with her life *experience*.

Kristen and Mike's divorce litigation dragged on for a year and a half after that, with Mike blaming her for all that had gone wrong, even the physical and emotional abuse. To add insult to injury, Mike postponed signing his extremely lucrative new contract until their divorce papers were signed. I guess he forgot about the sheets-for-curtains years.

Kristen's healing from all the layers of Mike's rejection was slow to get off the ground. It was nearly impossible to heal, she says, because she could not escape him. He was always in the paper, being talked about on TV or on the radio. And the fact that he had moved on with his life so quickly made the hurt even deeper. Around that time, he released his autobiography, and to Kristen's great shock, she wasn't even mentioned. Nine years together and not a single word. Kristen says she felt completely erased.

But God is good. It took time, but he did help Kristen get her life back. Oh, it wasn't easy. Those first few years were filled with plenty of self-help books, therapy, medication, support from her family, and lots of prayer. But here is the surprise: it was her therapist God used to plant the seed for her future story. He told her she would make a great therapist herself.

Fast-forward, and Kristen did, indeed, go back to school and now has her PhD. She found her purpose in helping others, not just with her professional training but with her life *experience.* She is a brilliant counselor to many people today because of her own pain and her capacity to understand theirs.

Oh, and I should mention one other thing. Kristen is now married to the most amazing man, and together they are raising their two young children. I don't know about you, but *that* is a team I can root for.

Camille

Camille is a fifty-six-year-old woman who has never been married or even asked. Not so long ago Camille would have been an unusual, perhaps suspect, member of society. But today, statistics indicate that she is far from alone. A *New York Times* analysis of the 2005 census found that more American women are living without a husband than with one. Fifty-one percent of American women are now single.[1]

Camille tells me that during her twenties and through her mid-thirties, she felt the desire, as most women do, to be married and in a loving relationship with a man. But she was not willing to settle for someone she did not truly love and who did not share her intellect and her love of God.

In her midthirties, Camille began to feel that, perhaps, something *was* wrong with her. Her friends had all married and were starting their families. She found herself always feeling as if she was tagging along and either going to parties alone or having to dredge up a date she did not particularly like. It was hard, she said, living in a world where everyone but her appeared to be paired up. When I asked her if she felt sad during that time, she said she didn't feel sad, more like *incomplete*.

And that, she said, is because society makes you feel as if you are not complete unless you have a mate. You are considered only half a person until you connect with the other half. The world happily accepts you if you have a mate, and if you don't, you always feel as if people are whispering and wondering why.

Magnify that a thousand times when it comes to the scrutiny of your family. Camille says there was a time she had to stop visiting her own grandmother, who rarely missed an opportunity to inquire why she was not yet married.

You may be wondering if Camille ever felt sort of cosmically rejected by never finding a husband with whom to share her life. The answer is, not a bit. That's because in her early forties, Camille finally did fall in love, not with a man but with the study of theology. She developed a passion for the Bible. And it became a powerful presence in her life and the source of her joy. Today, more than ten years later, Camille quit her job, finally made the decision to make a commitment, and currently is in her second year of seminary.

> Society makes you feel as if you are not complete unless you have a mate.

Camille says that, even though she has come to believe that God does not intend her to be married, it does not mean there are not times when she is "flat-out lonely." But what she has discovered is that marriage does not have to be the sole solution to loneliness or our desire to be in relationship.

The solution, she says, is in the body of Christ. Camille believes the church provides a place at the table for those not in *relationship* as the world defines it. And that is because she has found that intimacy in relationship does not always have to be sexual. If you think about it, all intimacy really involves is allowing yourself to be vulnerable, being with people who accept you for who and what you are, being with others who allow you to admit your failures and encourage you and love you in spite of yourself. That, Camille says, is *real intimacy* and what God offers her and all of us in his church, married or single.

It all boils down to three words, Camille says: "Love one another" (John 13:34).

Can a Woman Really Be Happy Without a Man?

You may be feeling a bit skeptical. Can a woman really find happiness without the presence of a man? Can God really replace the desire for a husband with something else? Are you ever *really* fulfilled without a mate?

The answer appears to be yes. In 2006, researchers in Australia, recognizing that a growing proportion of women were reaching older ages without having married or having children, set out to find if the assumptions about these women were true: they were lonely, impoverished, and unproductive. What they found was quite the contrary.

In a study of more than ten thousand husbandless and childless women, researchers found these women did not fare worse than their married, child-rearing counterparts. In fact, they were actually very social, successful, productive, happy women, who were *more* apt to volunteer and be social than those with families. Both of these things, researchers say, are related to *stronger* feelings of happiness in life.[2] How about that!

God's plan for Camille was different from his plan for Billie and Kristen. He provided them with loving husbands in the end. But if what God says is true, that he wants us *all* to have abundant, happy, fulfilled lives, then that is no less true for Camille than it is for Billie and Kristen. *Abundant* does not always have to be spelled M-A-N.

The Common Thread

Did you find the common thread that links these women's stories? Each one was "left at the altar" in one way or another. None of them accomplished their healing from rejection on their own. That, they all agree, would have been impossible. Each realized that she had come to the end of her own strength and could not deal with the rejection without divine intervention. Like most of us, they each had to face the truth that they were powerless to heal and move forward without God's help. As 2 Corinthians 1:9 says, "In our hearts we felt the sentence of death. But this happened that we might not rely on ourselves but on God, who raises the dead."

And the truly wonderful thing about God is, he always meets you where you are. It does not matter if you are in a hospital mental ward, as Billie was, or feeling desperate on your living room sofa, like Elizabeth, or isolated in a great big house all alone, like Kristen, or feeling incomplete and lonely, like Camille, God will meet you there. Whenever you are ready to completely turn things over to him, he's ready and more than willing to take over. There is nothing, not even shame, like Billie's, that could make him turn his back on you.

Also know that the way God deals with you may not look anything like the way he dealt with these women's pain or with mine. You are completely unique to God, and he will find the perfect, unique way to deal with your pain.

> The truly wonderful thing about God is, he always meets you where you are.

The God of the universe is the God of *miracles*. He knew the plans he had for Billie and Elizabeth and Kristen even before the men they loved rejected them. He knew how it would all work out. He knew Billie would have her second chance at life and make the most of it. He knew Elizabeth would be able to live the rest of her life in the assurance of Ernie's love. And he knew that Kristen would live her life fulfilling her true purpose of helping others, rather than living in the shadow of a husband. God knew how he would heal them and what he wanted to give them . . . just as he knows what he wants to give to you.

Nine

The Hole in My Heart

In the darkest night to be certain of the dawn . . .
to go through hell and to continue to trust
in the goodness of God—
this is the challenge and way.[1]

—ABRAHAM JOSHUA HESCHEL

It is too bad that when we are in the middle of something really horrible in our lives, God doesn't just come to earth, sit on the couch, lay out the blueprint for what's going to happen next, step-by-step, and explain in detail exactly how he's going to bring good out of all the bad. It would be seemingly so much easier if he worked that way, which is another question on my list of things I am going to ask him when I get to heaven. *Why?* If I had known how incredibly good my life would become *because* of getting left at the altar, I would have run out of that church myself!

A New Beginning

There really was not some *aha* moment when all of a sudden I *got it*, but over time I felt my dependence on self lessening and my dependence on God deepening. My faith evolved from simply *being a Christian* to having a real *relationship* with him. Many of the tools that I include in chapter 11 helped me along, especially my wonderful Bible study that forced me to dig into God's Word and his truth. And one day, when *he* was ready, when he knew *I* was ready, he nudged me back out into the world again—the world and the life he had prepared for me ahead of time.

> If I had known how incredibly good my life would become *because* of getting left at the altar, I would have run out of that church myself!

Flawed but Favored

I praise God that he inspired a Bible so full of flawed people just like me. Those people may have lived thousands of years before us, but it never ceases to amaze me how similar we are to them today. Take David, the king of Israel, for example. I don't know about you, but what he wrote in the Psalms sounds as modern and familiar to me as anything I read today, as anything I *feel* today. He absolutely captured what I was feeling in my own soul about God in the days and months after my rejection. Consider the following verses:

- Why, O LORD, do you stand far off? Why do you hide yourself in times of trouble? (10:1)

- How long, O LORD? Will you forget me forever? How long will you hide your face from me? How long must I wrestle with my thoughts and every day have sorrow in my heart? (13:1–2)

- My God, my God, why have you forsaken me? Why are you so far from saving me, so far from the words of my groaning? (22:1)

Even David, "a man after his own heart" (1 Sam. 13:14) felt at times that God had abandoned him.

Second Choice

Then there is Leah. Oh, how I relate to this woman! I completely *get* her. She is the poster child for unrequited, rejected love. And what an example she is to all of us who walk in similar shoes today.

Leah's story is in the book of Genesis. She was the older sister of Rachel and the first wife of Jacob. Jacob did not want to marry Leah; he wanted to marry Rachel, but their father tricked Jacob on Jacob and Rachel's wedding night by putting Leah into Jacob's bed. Jacob had already worked seven years for Rachel, so you can imagine he was not thrilled by this turn of events. Jacob did not love Leah, so he agreed to work seven *more* years so that he could also marry Rachel, the one he did love.

This story is heartbreaking on so many levels. First of all, the Bible describes Rachel as "lovely in form, and beautiful" (Gen. 29:17). The same verse describes Leah as having "weak eyes." Even her name breaks your heart because the meaning of *Leah* ranges from "cow" to "disgusted." Talk about an inferiority complex! First she had to grow up in the shadow of a beautiful, desirable, younger sister; then she had to live with a husband who, the Bible says, hated her and wanted someone else. And I think I had it bad.

That is a lot to bear, but the Scriptures also tell us something else: "The LORD saw that Leah was not loved" (Gen. 29:31). He *saw* her and was drawn to her suffering because *he* loved her even if Jacob did not. So God gave Leah a son. Who couldn't understand Leah's response to that: "Surely my husband will love me now" (v. 32)? She had given Jacob his firstborn son, so of course she thought he would now love her. Instead, nothing changed. He continued to reject her. Leah gave Jacob two more sons, but still he did not want her. Can you even imagine how this poor woman felt? The man she so loved, the father of her children, could never love her in the way she wanted. No matter what she did, how she tried to manipulate him and make him love her, he didn't. The tears she must have shed.

Then a wonderful thing happened. As Leah was pregnant with her fourth child, even though Jacob might not have loved her, she became aware that *God did.* God poured out his grace on sweet Leah and brought her to his side. In verse 35 she says, "This time I will praise the LORD." No more, "What can I do to make Jacob love me?" Instead she said simply, "This time I will praise the LORD."

We can only imagine how life changed for Leah after that. Instead of trying to find her worth in Jacob's love, she found it in God's. Her disappointment and heartache and feelings of rejection no doubt slowly evaporated as she worshiped God and found her joy in him. The happy ending to the story is that years later, after Rachel had died and then Leah, Jacob said to his sons on his deathbed, "I am about to be gathered to my people. Bury me with my fathers in the cave . . . which Abraham bought as a burial place . . . There Abraham and his wife Sarah were buried, there Isaac and his wife Rebekah were buried, and there I buried Leah" (Gen. 49:29–31). Jacob buried Leah where his ancestors had been buried, in a place of honor. And he wanted to be buried there with her.

That small passage tells us so much about how Leah must have changed in those years after she let go of Jacob and found her fulfillment in God. I imagine all the bitterness and unhappiness and resentment that had no doubt defined Leah were replaced by a

> Life changed for Leah after that. Instead of trying to find her worth in Jacob's love, she found it in God's.

peace, a gentleness, and a loving spirit. And I would guess that those weak eyes of hers became bright and sparkly and full of life. In the end, Jacob may have loved her just as God did. *Wow!* Now, that is a story I can relate to personally. Rejected by a man but loved by God. Man's rejection, God's protection. It's sad that Leah, like so many of us today, lived all those years not recognizing that the One who loved her was there all along.

Jessica

I met a woman who, sadly, has gone through a modern-day Leah experience of her own. Jessica and her husband had been married sixteen years when she discovered he was having an affair. That was painful enough, but Jessica would soon discover that her husband was not just involved with some random woman he met on a business trip out of town. No, he was cheating on her with Jessica's *best friend*. She and this woman had been so close for the past ten years that Jessica says they were *like sisters*.

For Jessica's sake I wish I could tell you that the affair had been a short-lived, thoughtless thing on his part, but it wasn't. Jessica's husband was in love with her best friend and wanted a divorce so that they could be together. This was a man to whom Jessica had devoted twenty years of her life, a man she had given three children, a man she loved and wanted to be with forever. She was devastated to learn that he no longer loved her. But can you even imagine the pain of a double betrayal, of knowing the two closest adults to you in the world had *both* betrayed you? And not only that, but the affair had been going on behind her back for four years.

Jessica's reaction was like any woman's would be. She began crying and stopped eating for days. She had lost not just a husband; she had lost also a best friend, a sister, the very person she *would* have turned to in her grief. And the jealousy! The jealousy in her heart, she says, was profound. She spent hours and hours hating herself for being older, shorter, heavier, and clearly not as sexually attractive as her best friend, who had stolen her husband's heart. And she spent weeks and months asking God why.

The good news is that Jessica did have a firm faith foundation to hold her up, even though, she admits, it was sometimes shaky. But she knew God would be faithful, and he was. She leaned on him as he gently encouraged her and gave her strength to take back her life. Her church friends and coworkers supported her, she took divorce recovery classes, and she went to the gym and made herself look and feel good again. It took two years, she says, but she did it. She took her life back.

As for forgiveness? Jessica is still working on that. Unfortunately her ex-husband and ex-best friend are still together, and because her children visit their father on alternate weekends, she has no choice but to have contact with them. But I expect the God of forgiveness will help her get to that point one day, as well, where she can forgive the betrayal of two of the people she had loved most in the world.

Left at the Cross

The story of God's love only becomes complete with the story of Jesus. Of all of us who have ever walked the earth and been rejected, he gets it like no one else. Because of that, he understands our suffering as no one else does.

Jesus had handpicked the twelve people he would trust to love him and carry on his message of hope and salvation. But on the night of his arrest, Jesus' best friends deserted him. All those people

> His rejection included being reviled, cursed, and stripped naked. Mine involved getting left at the altar in a very nice dress.

who just hours earlier had professed their undying devotion to him suddenly disappeared. You can feel Jesus' anguish there in the Garden of Gethsemane when in his darkest hour, he turned around and they were nowhere to be found (Matt. 26:55–56; Mark 14:48–51). When he had to carry his cross to Golgotha, none of his pals were there to encourage him or even walk silently beside him, much less help carry his load.

And when the Son of God was hanging by murderous spikes on that cross in the hot, Middle Eastern sun, beaten and bruised, the life seeping out of him, you could count on one hand the people who were there for him. There had been twelve disciples and countless followers during his vibrant ministry, but only his devoted mother, one disciple, an aunt, and one friend were there for him in the end (John 19:25–26). And let's not forget, these were people Jesus had come to *save*. He had come to earth in love to save the world from itself and to enable us to live with God forever, but the world rejected him and hanged him on a tree.

As for public humiliation? Mine happened only in Atlanta, Georgia, USA. His was for all eternity, recorded in the most widely read book in the history of mankind, read by literally billions of people down through the ages. His rejection included being reviled, cursed, and stripped naked. Mine involved getting left at the altar in a very nice dress.

Godly Grief

Jesus *gets* what it feels like to be rejected. But does he understand what it is like to hurt and grieve the physical loss of someone we love deep down? You bet. Remember the story of Lazarus? He and Jesus were very close friends. In fact, the Bible tells us, they were not just friends, but Jesus *loved* Lazarus and his whole family. One day Jesus was preaching and got a message that Lazarus was sick and asking him to come and make Lazarus better.

How did Jesus respond? Instead of going immediately to heal Lazarus, he waited two days before he left the place where he was teaching, and when he finally got to Lazarus's hometown, his friend was already dead. Obviously Jesus knew he was going to bring Lazarus back to life, but on seeing the grief of all his loved ones, and loving him so much himself, "Jesus wept" (John 11:35). The shortest verse in the Bible is, in so many ways, one of the most powerful, at least for me. It shows us that Jesus did feel human grief, the same way we do, and it indicates to us that when we pray to him today, he understands. I realize his love is not that girl-loses-boy or boy-loses-girl kind of grief, but I can assure you it is grief he understands just the same.

God also understands and reacts to our pain just as any loving parent would. Parents hurt when their children hurt. My mother will still tell you today that the day her child got left at the altar was the worst day of her life. And that's saying a lot. My mother lost her mother as a child, had a stepmother who was not so great, an alcoholic father, and a husband who left her, and she spent nearly all of her adult life disabled from arthritis. So when she says that her child's heartbreak was the worst of all that, you can see the magnitude of her love.

So now, think about our heavenly Father. He knew who we would be before time even began, created us in all our uniqueness, gave us people to love, watched us grow up, healed our wounds, delighted in our joy and our victories, laughed with us and cried with us . . . just like any loving parent does. That's how I know that when Lew left me at the altar that day, God was every bit as heartbroken as my mother. But he was equipped to help me deal with my pain in ways my earthly mother never could. He was with me when no one else was. He watched me every single moment, his spirit prayed for me, even when I couldn't, and he infused me with his strength, even when I would not ask. He sent loving arms to hold me and tender and patient hearts to comfort me. He was close to me when my heart was breaking, and he covered me with his mighty wings so I could find refuge.

A Breath of Hope

This loving Father did something else too. When he created me, he installed the one thing every human being needs to survive: hope. Even when I did not believe it was there, it was. On my darkest days of depression and feelings of hopelessness, there was this tiny, itsy, bitsy speck of hope that still burned in my soul, a flickering flame God kept burning even when I did not think he cared. He let me mourn. He let me grieve the loss of the love of my life. He even let me hate him and yell at him. But one day he gently blew his warm, Fatherly breath on that tiny flame of hope until it flared and grew, and he said, "Enough is enough. I have let you have your time to cry, be sad, and feel sorry for yourself, but you have mourned this man long enough. You have a life to live, young lady, and what a life I have in store for you!"

I wish I could tell you the exact moment that happened and give you

THE HOLE IN MY HEART

a blueprint for exactly how to get there yourself. I can promise you that God has such a moment planned for your life as well. All he wants is for us, like Leah, to acknowledge his presence in our lives and to trust him. That's why he makes such a big deal about trust in his Word. Over and over he begs us to trust him and promises us the most amazing peace if we will.

Again, I liken God to a loving Father, and in earthly terms I think of my own niece and nephews. I love them as much as I could love my own children. I want them to love me back and to trust me. But I can only imagine how hurt I would be if one of them did not trust me. For their entire lives I have been there, a third parent almost, the other person they could count on for whatever they need. So if one of them failed to trust me with any aspect of life, no matter how small, it would break my heart. And that is how God feels when we fail to trust him. It breaks his heart.

> "You have a life to live, young lady, and what a life I have in store for you!"

It also breaks his heart that we are so quick to buy into the lies of the deceiver when God has so clearly laid out the truth. The enemy wants us to be broken. God wants us to have abundant life. He plainly tells us in his Word, "For I know the plans I have for you . . . plans to *prosper you* and *not to harm you*" (Jer. 29:11, emphasis mine). Can't you just see him in heaven as excited as a parent on Christmas morning, knowing what he has in store and is wanting to give us? But God does not force himself on us; he allows us to choose. And that is where we come into the equation. Either we can choose to believe the lies about ourselves and about God, or we can choose to trust him. It really is as simple as that.

Living the Lie

Years ago I knew a woman who had gone through a nasty divorce. As is true of many women, her ego was left bruised and battered. It broke my heart watching her because long after she should have brushed off the lies her ex-husband had her believing about herself, she still clung to them. And when I say clung, I mean *clung*. Nothing anyone else could say could make this woman believe that she had a life beyond divorce waiting for her. She believed in God, but she did not *believe in* God's promises. I can't tell you how many times I heard her say that no one would ever love her or want her again, that she was too bitter about men after what happened to her, that men do not want women her age, that she was not the type of woman men are attracted to anyway, and on and on. Because she truly believed all of that, she never would even try to go out and date again, which just made her declarations a self-fulfilling prophecy. I tried for a long time, for years, to convince her otherwise and then concluded that all I could really do was pray for God to help her reject the lies she believed. I lost touch with that woman over time. I can only pray now that she sees herself much differently today and has gone on to feel like the special person I knew she was.

I happen to believe that most women choose to pull themselves out of that particular hell. Either they recognize the lies for what they are pretty quickly on their own, or they turn to God and let him bring them back to the truth.

The Rest of the Story

Before going on, I must finish the story of David, the psalmist. He may have been a king, but David was just like the rest of us. There were times he questioned God and wondered where he was. In Psalm 22 he is so low, in fact, that he compares himself to a worm (actually the one image in my own self-pity I didn't think of). He said, "Here I am, a nothing—an earthworm, something to step on, to squash" (v. 6 MSG). He goes on and on about how low he is, how the world hates him, how his strength is gone.

If you're beginning to feel really sorry for David and wondering where God was in David's suffering, remember that the twenty-second psalm comes right before the twenty-third, one of the most beloved, comforting pieces of poetry in all of literature. In Psalm 23, David paints a picture of God that, for me, is unparalleled in Scripture. He describes a Lord who acts as our loving Shepherd, giving us rest and strength and guidance even in the darkest hours of our lives. He is a Lord who leads us to still places and to quiet peace.

Yes, David gradually found his way out of his sorrow and back to his Lord. And eventually . . . so did I.

You can too.

Ten

The Man's Perspective

The hardest-learned lesson:
that people have only their kind of love to give,
not our kind.[1]

—MIGNON MCLAUGHLIN

There is one final kick-in-the-shins moment in my story I would be remiss if I did not share. Unfortunately, it came at a time when life was feeling pretty normal again. Lew was featured in *People* magazine as one of the year's "Most Eligible Bachelors." Imagine my surprise when there he was, on page 87, sitting in his home—*our* home—in a chair I had upholstered, holding a golf club, saying how he had once "almost made it to the altar." You can probably guess what I wanted to do with that golf club. I remember thinking that if it considered him an eligible bachelor, someone at *People* had not done her homework.

You know what I really wish? I wish that the article had gone on to explain what he was *thinking*. I have always wondered, *Did he not think I would see the magazine or at least hear about it? Did it ever occur to him that it might hurt me to see him talking about being single and brushing off in such a nonchalant way the heartbreaking way our engagement ended? Did he not think it would be more respectful, more considerate to someone he had professed to love to decline the offer to be one of* People *magazine's most eligible bachelors even though it was a very cool thing for him to do?*

Q & A

Talk with any woman who has been dumped by a man she loved or was hoping to (and I am talking about dating relationships here), and she will likely have been left with more questions than answers. Time and time again women tell me they just did not *understand* why he broke things off. They will then go on to recount pretty much the same type of story where everything seemed to be going so well, how they were having so much fun together, and how the relationship seemed to be heading somewhere when he just ended it.

Well, that started me thinking. Maybe it is time we got some answers. Surely we do not have to spend our singlehood in a perpetual state of bewilderment. There has to be some cause and effect, *something* going on in their minds to create this scenario that seems to get repeated much too often.

> Time and time again women tell me they just did not *understand* why he broke things off.

So, ladies, I have done some homework. I have talked with men who, strangely enough, were not so surprised by my queries on the subject and were quite willing to tell me what is actually going on in their brains and hearts when they dump us, often with no apparent reason. Let me give you a hint for what is to come: *apparent* is the key word.

What I am going to do is recount my conversations with several men who were kind enough to be open and honest on the matter. These are men of various ages and income levels, but basically, they are just men.

Patrick

Patrick is a thirty-three-year-old sales executive, cute and fun, and successful. He is the kind of guy girls like to take home to Mom. Patrick has never been married, but it is not because he is a commitment-phobe. He is not a serial dater; he is a serious guy when it comes to love. Right now, he is in a long-term relationship.

Even so, Patrick has had to do some rejecting in his life. And he says, despite what women think, it is never easy. For him, either he can see right off the bat that there is no chemistry and no point in moving forward, or if there is instant chemistry and interest, it will take him a little longer. Makes sense.

It is around the three- to four-month mark, Patrick says, that the man and woman both start to relax. They begin to let their guards down and allow their true selves to emerge. It's at this point, Patrick believes, that either they continue to move forward, or they back off. Backing off, in his experiences, was because he began to see "scary" things about the woman, such as a "mean streak" or a "psycho side" (his terms, not mine).

Patrick says his beef with a lot of women is that they tend to judge the man they are dating based on all the men from their past, particularly the ones who hurt them. Most guys, he says, are just trying to figure this love thing out, just as we women are, and most want the same thing in the end: to be in long-term committed relationships with women they truly love.

> Sixty percent are jerks, 40 percent are decent guys.

There are those guys, though, he had to admit, who are not so pure at heart. He says he has seen his own friends be jerks to women on more than one occasion. Lots of men, he admits, want to have their cake and eat it too. In fact, he would put the stats for all men at 60–40 percent. Sixty percent are jerks, 40 percent are decent guys. Let's hope he's wrong. But Patrick says when he sees his friends jerking women around, he flat out tells them, "There are nice ways to break things off. Maybe you need to think how *you* would like to be treated."

I like him.

Mark

Mark has been at this dating thing a lot longer than Patrick. He is forty-six years old and has also never been married. I would put Mark in a bit more of the playboy mold than Patrick but not in a bad way. This is a really good guy who loves God. He just also loves women.

When I asked Mark about the thought process when he is the one doing the rejecting, he immediately told me it is horrible, especially if you have been dating the woman for a while. He admits that he, like a lot of men, has stayed in relationships he knew were going nowhere longer than he should have because he did not want the woman to get hurt.

Mark tells me about one woman in particular. He says there was "enough there" to continue to go out after they met, but within three months, he knew she probably was not "the one." But again, he did not want to hurt her feelings, so rather than being a man about it and just telling her flat out, Mark says he began to be standoffish, physically and emotionally. He admittedly is not a good communicator. He says he was very relieved when she picked up on the vibes pretty quickly and asked him what was wrong so he could finally get it out and tell her the truth.

I like the fact that he can admit this.

What does Mark want you to know? Just as Patrick said, Mark believes that women have a misconception that it is easy for men to reject us. It's not, especially if there is a few months' history there. But he also wants us to know that *caring* for someone and enjoying her company do not mean he thinks she is the woman he wants to *marry*.

And that, my friend, may be the crux of the matter, the one thing we should take away. In our minds, caring for someone and enjoying his company are what *lead* to marriage, but for men, that may not always be the case.

Kevin

Kevin is going to serve as our "old married man," not old in terms of years because he is just forty-six years old, but old in terms of commitment—he has been married for a decade and now has some perspective on the whole dating and rejection thing.

Kevin tells me that in his past dating life, he was the "typical man." He would date a woman for a while, then break things off and move on to another. He says for him the easiest way to get over a breakup with one woman was to find another woman. As he looks back, Kevin says the reason he stayed in that pattern for so long was he just was not ready to get married. It would not have mattered if the world's most intelligent, kind-hearted supermodel had come along; he just was not ready.

Kevin, like Patrick and Mark, says he was terrible at breakups. He still sounds embarrassed today remembering how badly he handled them. He says the scenarios were always the same: he would date a woman, and after a while, she would want to know where the relationship was headed. Instead of being up-front about the fact that he was not ready to settle down, he would feel smothered, as if he couldn't breathe, and he would retreat. The more he retreated, the more the woman would pursue him until things became so unbearable, either she would call it off, or he would be forced to do it. And it was never pretty.

The interesting thing, Kevin says, is that he is not like that at all in business. Those decisions he makes with ease, ending business ties that are not working quickly and decisively. He is still pondering why he was not able to do the same with women.

So now that he has had time to reflect, Kevin has some interesting thoughts on relationships and breakups that he believes women need to hear. He says that life today has become so compressed, so fast, so all about self-gratification, that women do not allow relationships the proper time to *breathe*. He says

> Slow down! Let a relationship have time to develop. Let the man have time to let it all sink in.

he hears stories all the time of a woman going out with a man for just three or four weeks and behaving as if they are in a "relationship." "It is not a 'relationship,'" Kevin says, "*after three weeks!*"

Women, he believes, put much more emotional capital into the early stages of dating, the three- to six-month time frame. Women talk about it more, daydream about it more, discuss every aspect of it with friends. Men, meanwhile, are still just basically out for a good time. That is why, when it feels as if men move on so much quicker after a breakup, it is because they generally did not have that much emotional capital invested. If, however, a guy does feel upset over things, it is because he did. "Don't forget," Kevin says, "men have feelings too."

The bottom line for Kevin, and the advice he has for his single female friends, is to slow down! Let a relationship have time to develop. Let the man have time to let it all sink in. Keep having fun and enjoying each other's company. And remember that, unlike most women, men are either ready to settle down or they are not. If they are not, never feel badly about yourself when things don't work out. It wasn't you. It was probably just bad timing.

Evan Katz: Online Dating Consultant and One Straight Talker

Well! Lest there be any confusion or misunderstanding on the matter of men rejecting women, you need to hear from Evan. He is as honest and straightforward on the matter as any man you will ever talk to about it. Buck up for this one, ladies; he does not hold back.

When I asked Evan why it seems that men have such an easy time breaking things off with women, he had one word: *hypocrisy*. And he did not say it nicely. Evan says he is fed up with this man-versus-woman thing that women have created. It is a people-versus-people thing, and if we don't think men get hurt in relationships, we are wrong. Women detach just as easily, he says; he sees it in his line of work all the time. And he is tired of women pointing fingers.

It is not what men do to women, Evan says; it is what *people do to people.*

What he will admit to is that men do tend to avoid "the conversation." It is very uncomfortable for a man to have to tell you something you obviously are not going to want to hear. So rather than sit down for a heart-to-heart emotional experience with you, he will simply be rude and hope you get it. For him, that is a lot easier than watching you cry your eyes out.

> Every man who ends things with a woman has a reason. It is not irrational. It makes sense to *him.*

And besides, he says, do women *really* want to hear things like . . .

- "I've just been going through the motions with you; I'm actually not feeling it."

- "I'm just not that physically attracted to you."

- "I don't find your friends very interesting."

- "Your family annoys me."

He does have a point. In the end, and here is the bottom line according to Evan: Does it really matter what the reason is? Women always seem to want *closure and clarity,* but what purpose does it really serve? You are still in the same place. He could send you a love note and flowers, says Evan, but you are still broken up. You may have solved the mystery of why, but so what?

Everybody, he says, sees the world through his own prism. And every man who ends things with a woman has a reason. It is not irrational. It makes sense to *him*.

Evan's advice to women: turn things around. It is all about understanding one another and recognizing, "If you are really honest, you have probably done the same thing to some guy in the past. Whether you rejected him the first time he asked you out after meeting at a party or after a few dates when you decided he wasn't your type, or after a few months when you had more serious concerns, you had your reasons too."

Evan says women just need to be fair. We are all just people being people.

From the Pros

That may have been tough to hear, but I think Evan has some very valid points. But to be fair to everybody, we really should hear what trained, unbiased therapists have to say on the subject of how men and women handle relationships, particularly for our purposes, the ending of them, the rejection. And it appears to be all in the wiring.

The first thing we need to keep in mind is that therapists are not saying that *all men* or *all women* behave the same way in the breakup of relationships. In fact, therapists say, research has shown that it is actually about 85 percent of men and 85 percent of women who will have the same types of reactions.

So it all begins, the professionals tell me, with how men and women tend to define themselves. Women do it through their relationships, men through their successes, such as their careers, how much money they make, or how good they are at golf. And that is not just because of how we are genetically configured but also our socialization.

Check out any third-grade playground. Harvard clinical and social psychologist Carol Gilligan, in doing research for her landmark book *In a Different Voice*, found that the differences between men and women actually appear when we are quite young. She found that the way little girls talk and conduct themselves is relational, based more on the interests of others, rather than themselves, while little boys are more self-focused, more competitive. An example: When boys have a dispute while they're playing, they actively resolve it and keep playing. Girls, however, will quit playing in order to protect the relationship. To us women, nothing is more important than the relationship.[2]

One of my favorite books of all time is Deborah Tannen's *You Just Don't Understand*. The Georgetown University PhD is a linguistics expert, who has written extensively on the subject of how men and women communicate. She says researchers have found gender differences in the way children talk as young as three. Three!

As children grow up, she says this:

Boys tend to play outside, in large groups that are hierarchically structured. Their groups have a leader, who tells others what to do and how to do it and resists doing what other boys propose. It is by giving orders and making them stick that high status is negotiated. Boys' games have winners and losers.

Girls, on the other hand, play in small groups or in pairs; the center of a girl's social life is a best friend. Within the group, intimacy is key: Differentiation is measured by relative closeness. Many of their [girls'] activities [such as playing house] do not have winners or losers.[3]

So what does any of that have to do with relationships and rejection? Tannen says:

The boys' play illuminates why men would be on the lookout for signs they are being put down or told what to do. The chief commodity that is bartered in the boys' hierarchical world is status, and the way to achieve and maintain status is to give orders and get others to follow them. A boy in a low-status position finds himself being pushed around.

The chief commodity that is bartered in the girls' community is intimacy.[4]

The Waffle Effect

Men, according to therapists, also tend to compartmentalize their lives. We hear this all the time, but it is true, and apparently there is actual research to back it up. They have even coined a term for it: the *waffle effect*. The term reflects the tiny individual squares that make up a waffle.

So when men break things off in a relationship, it is much easier for them to seal off that compartment and turn to another. That is why it is so frustrating to women when we are crying our eyes out, refusing to leave our apartments, and they are moving on with their lives. We want *them* to be crying their eyes out and refusing to leave their apartments too. To us, that feels as if we meant nothing to them at all since they so easily disengaged. But that is not necessarily how they feel at all. It is just intrinsically easier for them to move on to other areas of their lives.

The Real Culprit

Todd Sandel, a Christian counselor who heads the Lifegate Counseling Center in Atlanta, has a really interesting take on all of this. He believes that *fear* is actually the root of it all. And the genesis of that is in . . . Genesis.

Fear, Sandel says, entered humanity in the Garden of Eden after Adam and Eve ate the fruit God had told them not to eat. The second they did it, they were afraid. And their response to the fear was to cover their shame, avoid/escape into hiding, and blame someone else for what they had done. After that, fear was hard-wired into humanity.

Today, both men and women have fear, but it is the things we fear that make us different:

- Women, therapists say, tend to fear being devalued, unloved, insignificant, alone, disconnected, and unappreciated.
- Men fear being inadequate, not good enough, ineffective, or failures.

So while women are *feeling* the pain of a breakup because we are afraid we are always going to be unloved and alone, Sandel says it's very possible that most men often sweep whatever negative feelings they have about it under the rug. For them to actually *face it* would mean recognizing an inadequacy or failure and admitting any shame for not making the relationship work or that they were ineffective or not good enough in some way. He says most men probably do not even know why they are reacting the way they are . . . if that makes you feel any better.[5]

Poignant Points

All of these men, the professional daters and the professional therapists, are telling us some poignant things that women today truly need to hear. Let's sum them up and, perhaps, posting them on the refrigerator would be in order:

1. Women need to stop the male bashing. It is not an us-against-them thing. We are all just human beings trying to navigate the same rocky waters of love, albeit in very different ways.

2. Contrary to what we feel, men do have valid reasons *for them* for ending relationships, whether they are able to express them in ways we want to hear or not.

3. Also, contrary to what we often believe, even though men do not always show it, breakups do affect them; they just don't send them into therapy.

4. Be mindful of signals a man may be giving that he is backing off. Watch what he *does*, not just what he *says*. If he calls but does not make plans to see you, that's because he does not want to see you. If he begins to e-mail rather than have personal contact on the phone, that's generally a good indication he may not be feeling as excited about things as you are. All of the men I interviewed told

me they believe women know this anyway, but they often choose to ignore the signs.

5. Men and women are genetically different by God's design, and we are socialized differently. That means the way we respond to situations is going to be different. We need to recognize that and try to understand each other better.

6. All human beings operate from fear. But what men and women fear is different. Women cannot let their fears of being alone and unloved paralyze them and prevent them from getting over the rejection and moving forward. If a man rejects you, that does not mean the entire male gender is going to reject you forever until you are too old and tired to care.

In the end, Sandel says, the relationships that go on to make it are the ones that are operating as God patterned for us in the Trinity: God the Father, the Son, and the Holy Spirit, separate but in union together. Yes, joined together as Jesus said as "one flesh" but also finding happiness and purpose as *individuals*. Relationships work better that way, Sandel has found, because people will always disappoint and hurt us. No one person can ever meet all of our needs. Our only true secure attachment, as the psalmist writes, is in God: "He alone is my rock and my salvation" (Ps. 62:2).

Doesn't it feel good to finally get some insight from the other side?

Eleven

Moving On!

I believe that God is in me
as the sun is in the color and fragrance of a flower—
the Light in my darkness, the Voice in my silence.

—HELEN KELLER, *MY LATER LIFE*

As the weeks of my recovery from grief and pain turned into months, I did smile again, laughed even, and the first thing I thought about when I woke up was not always Lew. Nearly a year later my television station offered me an extended contract with a hefty pay raise, and for the first time in a long time I began to feel hopeful. I was enjoying my career, that part of my life again, and I was beginning to regain a small sense of myself.

Then four months later, my news director asked me to lunch— which is almost never good—to tell me that the station was not happy having two women anchor the five o'clock news, and I would be moving to weekends. I could not believe what I was hearing. *Back to weekends!* That was a shift I thought I would never have to work again and a

135

major step backward in my career. Plus, let's face it, that meant no weekend nights to go on dates.

I immediately said I would not do it. He asked me to at least give it some thought over the weekend. But less than twenty-four hours later, I told him I had made up my mind, and I wanted out of my contract. To say I was stunned is an understatement. That was the one area of my life where I was regaining my equilibrium. Now it, too, was gone. I felt as if the final piece of the foundation had been kicked out from under me. No husband and now no job. Self-pity does not even begin to describe my state of mind.

Scare on the Air

Do you know how you *know* things are really bad? When your mom tells you, "At least you've got your health." She, of all people, knew that to be true; after all, she had spent a third of her life in a wheelchair, but it seemed to me that everybody my age was healthy. Saying I was fit was not saying a lot. But wouldn't you know it, not long after my sudden unemployment, I began to lose weight. For months I chalked it up to all the stress of the past few years, but by fall I realized something was really wrong. The weight loss by then was accompanied by frequent heart palpitations and irritation in my eyes, and I was incredibly emotional.

I had begun freelance anchoring at CNN and could see in the monitor in the studio that I didn't look like myself. My face was gaunt, and even with all the television makeup, I did not look well. It all came to a head one evening when I was solo anchoring as I began reading the top stories. My heart began racing, my palms sweating, and the words just stopped coming. I could not catch my breath, and I began to hyperventilate. When we went into a sound bite, I told my producer he would have to go to a commercial, I could not continue. It occurred to me that I was finally having a nervous breakdown. And I was terribly disappointed that it was on national television.

I was diagnosed a short time later with Graves' disease, a thyroid disease that causes the thyroid—the gland that controls how the body works—to go into overdrive. My doctor told me it was clearly brought on by stress. At the turn of the twentieth century, he said, it used to kill people, mostly women, because the heart can only beat that fast for so long without giving out. Fortunately, today the prognosis is not as bad as the name of the disease would lead you to believe, and I was easily treated. But my, how life had changed in two short years!

I had gone from being a successful television anchor, secure professionally and financially and on the verge of settling down with a man I adored, who would be the father of my perfect, adorable children, to a woman broken in every way possible—physically, financially, and emotionally. I was weak, worn-out, hopeless, and helpless. I was as low as a person can be. But the fact that I am writing this, healed and happy, is proof that either we can choose to be miserable forever, or we can choose to claim God's promises. I chose the latter.

Tools for Thriving

Right now, as you read this, you may also feel pretty weak, worn-out, hopeless, and helpless. But trust me; God does some of his best work when we are there. I should know! When we are weak but somehow, amazingly, manage to survive and even thrive, it has to be God who makes it happen. We finally realize we are powerless without him, and he gets the credit and the glory. That's how it works.

What I have done is compile ten tools for healing and ten tools for moving forward that worked for me. These are not some platitudes by a preacher in a pulpit, who has been married to the same woman for thirty-five years, or a therapist who has studied lots of books on the subject. They are real-life, practical tools shown by God to someone who had to learn and perfect them the hard way. I am praying that they will work for you as well.

Tools for Healing

1. **Know that God cares.** Right now, you may not feel it; you may be angry with him, but he has heard it all before, and he is big enough to deal with that. If you can know only *intellectually* that God cares, even though you do not feel it in your heart, that's okay; it's a start. I promise you that one day you will look back on this time and realize that he was there all along, and you will then be able to see the countless ways he held you up and comforted you. As Psalm 23 says so well, "Even though I walk through the valley of the shadow of death, I will fear no evil, for you are with me." He will probably use other people or other experiences to show you his presence, and there is no telling what devices he will use because he has a big arsenal. Just know that he is there in your suffering and will bring good out of this bad.

2. **Realize it's okay to mourn.** As I told you earlier, when Lew left, he might as well have died because that is how horrible I felt,

which is why I believe you have to give yourself permission and time to mourn the one who has rejected you. Someone you loved or were hoping to love is gone and is not coming back. Your dreams for the future (with him) have also died. This is not something to be taken lightly. Those who say men are like buses, because there will always be another one, may be right, but this is not the time to be flippant. This is a serious loss that has hurt you deeply, and you have to give it the weight it deserves. Facing it, dealing with it, is the only way to begin to move forward. "There is a time for everything . . . a time to weep and a time to laugh, a time to mourn and a time to dance" (Eccl. 3:1, 4).

3. **Allow family and friends to comfort you.** Don't do what I did and shut people out by refusing to answer the phone or return phone calls or by never going out. Those people who are calling and wanting to see you are the hands and feet of God, doing what he has called them to do, which is to show you his presence in a physical way. As Romans 10:15 says, "How beautiful are the feet of those who bring good news!"

Let them lend ears to listen, shoulders to cry on; let them cook dinner, take the kids overnight. Love is a great salve. And it is a major way that God is trying to show you he cares. These are also the people who care about you most, so they don't mind that your eyes are nearly swollen shut from crying, that you are completely immersed in self-pity, or that you don't care about the cute thing their little Johnny did at school today. This is all about you right now, and that's okay.

4. **Don't mourn too long.** After a while those people who have

been holding you up will need to get back to their own lives and expect you to start standing on your own two feet again. Not only that, but too much mourning will turn you completely inward, which can only lead to prolonged self-pity. And self-pity is a very unattractive, unsympathetic trait to develop. You will find that people will support you in your sadness, but self-pity not so much. Besides, you do not want to see yourself as a victim. You may be a lot of things right now, but never, ever see yourself as a victim. Victims have no control over what happens to them, and you, my dear, most certainly do. You can *choose* to take hold right now, turn this pain over to God, and let him lead you out of this state of mind.

How long is too long to mourn? Therapists have differing views on the correct timetable, if there is one. Some say it is half the time you were together; some say it depends on how much your identity was wrapped up in the other person. For me, I just knew when mourning was turning into self-pity. As God himself promises, "I will turn their mourning into gladness; I will give them comfort and joy instead of sorrow" (Jer. 31:13).

5. **Focus on the truth.** Boy, this was a big one for me. Why, oh why, after he left, did I only dwell on the good memories and the happy times? All that did was cause me to cry more. Why didn't I face the truth of the situation? I have talked to many women who say they did exactly the same thing when they were rejected, which is why I am convinced it must be something in our wiring.

As weird as it sounds, if you can focus on the truthful negative aspects of the relationship, it really will end the mourning period faster and help you remember the relationship *as it really was,* not the fairy tale you *wanted it to become.* The Bible says, "Then you will know the truth, and the truth will set you free" (John 8:32). However, if this was someone for whom you had hopes for a long-term relationship, facing the negatives may be harder to do since you may not have had many negative experiences. But to begin healing, you must focus on the truth that he did not perceive things the same way you did, for whatever reason. It just was not a good fit for him. In this case, there *will* be another bus!

6. **Don't waste valuable time plotting ways to get him back.** This, of course, is coming from the woman who actually got back together with the man who left her at the altar. I honestly thought we could work through all the pain he had caused me, my family would forgive and forget, and we would all live happily ever after. Instead, I spent valuable time focusing on a relationship that never was going to happen when I should have been moving in a different direction. I would give anything to have those months and, yes, years back.

What I have learned is that if a man has made the decision to leave the relationship, it is probably painful for him as well. For him to actually go through with it, he is very serious because men do not like pain. If you had hopes for a relationship with someone who never called you back, obviously he wants to move on and find the one who does click for him. Either way, let him go. Life is short and chances are you would spend lots of time and energy and never win him back anyway, ending up feeling a lot worse than you do now. This is time you could spend finding the one who does want you, whom God wants for you. And he *is* out there. As a friend of mine says, "Life is short, so eat dessert first!" Don't miss out on the most delicious part of life by getting stuck in the spinach.

7. **Get back into your routine quickly.** When I finally mustered up the courage to go back to work, I had to pretend to be perky on the air. And then one day, I realized I wasn't pretending anymore. Going back to work was the best thing I did to get on with life. If nothing else, it will be eight or nine hours of your day when you are not feeling entirely miserable by focusing on what you lost. So get back to doing what you normally do. Besides work, do you normally go to the gym, do volunteer work, have a weekly lunch with friends? Then do those things.

However, you will want to stay away from any part of your routine that involved the one who rejected you. If he goes to your church, go to a different service; if he works out at your gym, find a new one. The last thing you need is to keep running into him. You will never be able to heal and move forward if he is constantly in your orbit. If you have children he must pick up and drop off every week, arrange to have as little contact as possible.

As usual, God said it best in Philippians 3:13–14: "Forgetting what is behind and straining toward what is ahead, I press on toward the goal to win the prize for which God has called me heavenward in Christ Jesus."

8. **Find a godly counselor.** This has to be a person who can really be honest and objective about you and your situation. Do not let

yourself gravitate to friends who will enable your feelings of sadness. I found myself wanting to be only with the people who didn't hate Lew so I could talk with them, and they would be sympathetic to the reasons I still loved him and wanted him back. These people mean well, but they just want what they think *you* want and what will make you happy.

It is so much better if you can find someone who is grounded in God's principles, who will advise you in ways that will enable your healing and moving forward. It needs to be someone who can see the situation through objective, unemotional eyes. This does not have to be a professional therapist; it could also be a pastor, a Bible study leader, or someone at work. The only criterion is that he or she must be fluent in God's Word and able to be completely honest and objective. As Psalm 119:107 in *The Message* says, "Everything's falling apart on me, GOD; put me together again with your Word."

9. **Stay in constant contact with God.** God tells us to pray continually, in all circumstances, and yes, that means even when we have been rejected. Prayer keeps the conversation with God going, and he will answer those prayers. Remember, *before you call him* he will answer, and while you are still speaking, he will hear you (Isa. 65:24). I also suggest getting a really good daily devotional to get you in the routine of talking to God, if you don't already do that. And memorize some scriptures that are meaningful to you, scriptures that speak to the pain you are in right now. Being able to call them up in the middle of the day

when you feel sad is a great tool. I did not do that in the early months after being left at the altar because I was so angry with God. I so wish I had. But here is one you might try to remember right now: "The LORD is close to the brokenhearted and saves those who are crushed in spirit" (Ps. 34:18).

10. **Turn off the deceiver's voice.** You are now fertile ground for the enemy, who tries to derail your healing and continues to try to separate you from God. When those negative thoughts, such as *you aren't good enough*, or *you're a failure*, come into your mind, deliberately stop them. You can control your mind and your thoughts. The deceiver will try to keep you down because if you do get up with God's help, guess who gets the glory? God. And the last thing the enemy wants is for God's goodness and faithfulness to shine. As 1 Peter 5:8–9 says, "Be self-controlled and alert. Your enemy the devil prowls around like a roaring lion looking for someone to devour. Resist him, standing firm in the faith."

Tools for Moving On

After your healing is well under way, and when life begins to feel normal again, you will start having those wonderful, long-forgotten pangs of actually *wanting* to find out what God has in store for you. You will start feeling *excited* about all of life's prospects, and chances are, if you are like me, you will want to find the real person with whom you are meant to be. So here are my tried-and-true tools for doing just that:

1. **Get into a good women's Bible study or small group.** Once you start to feel normal again, you may be tempted to think you can

turn God loose and handle things on your own once again. *Nothing could be farther from the truth.* This was a critical tool in my own moving forward. I joined a local chapter of Bible Study Fellowship (BSF), a nationwide Bible study. It kept me firmly tied to God's Word with women who shared my newfound passion for knowing him. While you do not have to share your story with other women if you don't want to, it is a place where you will feel safe because, I promise you, every woman in that room has or will have pain in her life.

2. **Lose the fear.** Chances are the one thing you wanted before your rejection is the same thing you want now—someone to love. And you are going to be scared to death at the mere thought of getting back out there and finding him. It takes a lot of courage, especially since you now feel you have REJECTED stamped on your forehead. Fear—there's that word again—will be another tool the deceiver uses to try to keep you isolated and alone. You must work through it. I loathe blind dates. But I had to make myself endure them. That may be your path, too, or you may find that you would rather meet people in other ways, such as at church or in night classes. Whatever you feel comfortable with is fine, just do something to get yourself back out there. And as for the fear of being rejected again, that may never fully go away. But I am convinced that if God has, indeed, set someone aside for you, that man will never make you feel afraid.

3. **Don't talk about your rejection when you do start dating.** Yes, your rejection has been your whole life lately, but it has not been your date's. He probably will not be interested in your sad story,

and it will only make you look as if you are still tied to that past relationship and not open to a new one. For me, this was a little hard, since many people had heard about my getting left at the altar. People do find that fascinating, so I would quickly address it, try to make a joke about it, and steer the conversation elsewhere. Politics is always good.

4. **Realize that you will inevitably compare every man who comes along to the one who rejected you.** At least initially. And then, only the good parts, not the bad ones. This is simply not fair to any person. Yes, you can look for the same good, healthy qualities you loved in that other person, but try to find new things to love in someone else. When I started dating again, I remember comparing everybody to Lew: Was this new guy as smart, as witty, as successful? Would we share the same interests/politics/work ethic? What I should have been pondering were questions such as these: Does this new guy love God as I do? Does he share the same goals for his life, such as marriage and children? Will he be the type to stick it out in thick or thin? Will he still love me when I'm old? Yes, chemistry and similar interests are important, but in mature, adult, lasting, God-inspired relationships, the latter questions are what matter most.

5. **Don't make it a priority or become obsessed with replacing that person who rejected you.** This is not healthy. Men read desperation like the morning paper. God really does have the reins on this one. Just chill. Getting out there and being willing to meet new people is one thing. Obsessing about meeting a man is another. The best way to attract someone is to be independent and happy

with your own life. People like that. They want to be around that. And never forget that no person can make you feel complete. God never, despite what Renee Zellweger tells Tom Cruise in *Jerry Maguire*, wants someone else to *complete us*.

6. **Develop patience.** If you can learn to be patient and wait on the Lord with this relationship you want so much, you will have gained something incredibly valuable for all areas of your life as you move forward. Patience is nothing more than trusting God with what you desire. It is being able to completely let go and to relax. Remember, God's Word says, "Delight yourself in the LORD and he will give you the desires of your heart" (Ps. 37:4). I was the most impatient person before my rejection. Since then I have spent years trying to develop patience, and I am happy to tell you that, while I haven't perfected this particular fruit of the Spirit, I am better at it. I even find I am having less road rage. Waiting for someone new to love is hard. God's timing is almost never our timing, but it is always perfect.

7. **Beware of loneliness.** This is really important, especially if you were in your former relationship a long time. If you are used to having someone around, this may be one of the hardest things you are dealing with now. Loneliness is a terrible feeling, and it can prompt us to do things we know we shouldn't or be with people we shouldn't. Guard yourself against the temptation to be with someone who you know is not healthy for you or someone in whom you know there is no future simply because you do not want to be alone. Fill this time with other endeavors or other people, and be aware that God may be using this lonely time to

work out other purposes in your life that have nothing to do with romantic love.

8. **Continue to reject the deceiver's lies.** Do not think for a second that, since you are getting on with your life, the enemy will now move on to someone else. He is there and as active as ever; he just has a new set of lies to tell you. He may now try to convince you that this lonely period is proof that you will never find "the one." He will whisper such lies as, "You are too scared to be loved again," or "You are too old," or "Every good man's already paired up with someone else." Just as before, turn off the lies and cling to God's truth.

9. **Realize that you may very well be rejected again.** This may sound negative and discouraging, but it's not. It is an important thing to process so that you can put any future rejection in proper perspective. After Lew left, anytime someone I met did not call me back after a date, I felt really rejected even if I didn't really like him either. The deceiver would start whispering the lie that no one was ever going to love me again. That, unfortunately, is one of the scars of rejection. Every time it happens, even in a small way, it tends to pile on top of all the other rejections in your past and make you feel worse than ever.

When it happens to you, and it likely will, please do not let that stop you from trying because here is what I have learned after plenty of experience: dating for a mate is like trying to find the perfect black dress. You try on a lot of black dresses until you find the perfect one. *It is not personal.* There was nothing wrong with any of those other black dresses; they were perfectly fine black dresses; they just were not exactly the right black dress *for you*. That person across the table, just like you, is trying to find the perfect fit for him. If, after one or two or even four or five dates, he decides you are not the one, it may feel like it, but it is not a rejection of you. It is just not the right fit. When it happens, if it does, repeat these words: man's rejection, God's protection.

10. **Allow God to reveal to you the exciting plan he has in store for you.** As you stay in prayer and in his Word, also open your heart and mind to whatever God's plan for you is. It may be that God keeps you going in the same direction you were in before your rejection. It may be that he takes you on a path you have never dreamed of before. He may have something else he wants for you to do, something that will fulfill you in ways you cannot even imagine. But if he does send that man you have been praying for, just know that he may not come in the package you are expecting or that you are used to seeing. In fact, he may be the last person you would dream up. That is the neat thing about God. He is capable of the most amazing surprises. This is the God who created you, the God who has a plan and a purpose designed *just for you*. So open your heart and let him show you what marvelous things he has in store.

I don't just *think* these tools work, ladies; I *know* they work because they absolutely worked for me. They allowed me to heal and get on with my life and centered me for whatever was to come. Always remember the first step is recognizing that God is with you; he has not rejected you. Everything else will flow from there. Your tools may vary from mine; there might be things you need to work on that I did not or vice versa. My point is to make sure that God and his principles are at the center of any healing and moving-forward manual you create for yourself. And stick with them! Trust me; it is easy to stray. Pray for him to help you, and he will.

Twelve

Laugh Again, Love Again

It was a beautiful morning that day in late September.

Of course, it always seems to be a beautiful day when you are in love.

The sky is a little bluer, the birds' chirping a little sweeter,
*   your favorite songs always on the radio.*

But that day in late September was more beautiful than all the others
*   because this was the day of my magical wedding.*

We all awoke that day on St. Simons Island a little groggy from the
*   night before.*

The rehearsal and dinner had gone on much too late, but it had been so
*   much fun and so full of joy that no one wanted to say good-night.*
*   There had been lots of laughter and love. Oh, the love! I don't think*
*   I've ever felt such love for the people all around me, especially for*
*   "him" and for God, who had finally brought me full circle.*

When I arrived at the tiny chapel, nestled in the shade of the moss-covered
*   oak trees, the sight of it nearly took my breath away.*

It was quaint and lovely, a place obviously blessed by God,
*   the perfect place for us to begin our lives together.*

No hint of pretention, simple and uncomplicated, just like my life had become.

Inside, I am told, he has already arrived. In fact, so anxious to see his
  bride, he arrived admittedly early. The chapel's old wooden pews (there
  aren't many) are filled with the smiling faces of the people I love most.
  My family, my mother (who is feeling wonderful today), my sister and
  niece, who will be my bridesmaids, and my brother, who will walk me
  down the aisle. There are friends, of course, but only the dearest ones. I
  think they are even happier about this day than I.
And as I stand at the back of the church I see him.
He is beaming.
As he sees me for the first time, his eyes take on a glimmer that I hope will
  never fade.
He is a man in love,
  a man who has found the person he, too, has prayed to find for so long.
As the music from the tiny piano begins, there is one more thing I notice—
  the smell of the gardenias blooming outside.
And the fragrance is wonderful . . .

After the thyroid disease scare and a brief stint in politics, I knew
that what I really wanted to do was to get back to the career I loved,
back to television. But after all I had been through, the last thing I
wanted to do was go back to covering murders and fires. Something
more uplifting was what I had in mind, but I was not sure exactly what
that was, much less how to get there.

Then I remembered an agent I had crossed paths with years before,
who was working in the entertainment field, and I decided to give her
a call. I flew out to L.A., and I will never forget the look on her face
when I told her what I had been up to in the past few years. She was

completely entranced by my story of being left at the altar, and the first thing out of her mouth when I was finished was, "Kimberley, you have got to use that story to get your next job!"

I sat there in confused bemusement until she explained. "Make a resume tape," she said, "describing what happened, in the same self-deprecating, funny way you just told me. Use the story to move forward. It will make you different from everybody else out there and show that you can do more than serious news."

I thanked her for her time, wondering what had happened to her previous good judgment, and thinking I had better find an agent who wasn't nuts, until I got on the plane and suddenly realized how utterly brilliant it was. I could turn this lemon of a chapter of my life into lemonade and set myself apart as someone creative and daring and worthy of a shot. By the time I got back to Atlanta, I had written my script.

A good friend of mine, a producer and photographer with whom I had previously worked, had just started his own production company and graciously agreed to shoot and edit my tape. We decided to do it—get this—inside a church, with my describing how I had been left at the altar, about the final blow of Lew's appearing in *People* magazine, and how I was excited about moving forward into a new chapter of my life. It was sad and yet funny, and it worked.

Back in the Spotlight

Not long after that, I got a call from the programming director at the ABC affiliate in Atlanta where I had worked in news years before, saying he was thinking of starting a new news and entertainment show, and he asked if I would be interested in anchoring it. Six months later, we started our show. I had to completely step out in faith because I had no contract and no guarantee of a paycheck; we literally stayed on the air week to week to see if people would watch. They did. From almost our very first night, we beat the other shows in our time period. The show was a success, and it felt good to be back.

I wish I could tell you at that point, all the Lew stuff was finally behind me, that getting this new gig in TV ended up being symbolic for the closing of one door and the opening of another. It wasn't. Just a few months after we started our show, a local newspaper, *The Atlanta Journal-Constitution*, featured a story on me about my being back on the air, the new show, and how I had made the resume tape using the story of my rejection to help get the job. It took about two days for that article to grab the attention of a producer at ABC's *Good Morning America*, who then called and said the show wanted to do a story— about my story. Diane Sawyer later did another piece for a *Primetime* special about weddings. Mine was the sad one. By the time *GMA* did its third piece, updating my life after being left at the altar, I could see my story not only was resonating with people everywhere—not just in Atlanta—but also I probably would never be able to completely leave behind that chapter of my life with Lew.

So here I am seven years later. Our show is still on the air, and now I'm not only anchoring the show but also writing and producing it. I have never had so much fun in my life. It is truly my dream job. No more covering the depressing news of murders and fires. This show is interesting, informative, entertaining, and mostly uplifting, and I would never, ever be doing it had Lew not left me at the altar. I would still be immersed in doing the regular news of the day and not nearly as fulfilled creatively as I am today. For that I am thankful.

If only the dating part of my new life had been as easy . . .

Back in the Game

When I finally did start going out again, I inevitably compared every man I dated with Lew. The good Lew, not the bad Lew. So in the beginning, nobody lived up to the ideal I still believed I had lost. Either they were not smart enough or funny enough or didn't *get me* as he did. I would love to go back and date some of those men over again now because one of them may have been just the right fit.

My new dating life, which I was trying to incorporate into my new faith life, was not much fun in the beginning. When word got out that I was ready to get back out there, everybody and their uncle had someone to fix me up with on a blind date. It was an excruciating process but one I knew I needed to endure if I was ever going to find someone new to love.

I went on every single blind date I was offered, and even though I was praying really hard for courage, I dreaded each one. I would spend the entire week imagining the discomfort of driving to the restaurant and that awkward first ten seconds when we would meet. (Remember, I am on TV, so they had probably already checked me out. I, however, did not have the same luxury.) I would dread the thought of sharing a meal with a man I did not know and have to start all over with the

"What do you do? Where did you grow up?" conversation. I would have absolutely no expectation that this man would be anybody I would like or who would like me.

And then there was the uncomfortable good-night ritual when no one knows what to say or do. If I don't like him, how do I be polite but not encourage him? If I do like him, I'll have to go through all the anxiety of wondering if he'll ever call me back. It still gives me nightmares.

Time went by, and after I had gone through all the eligible men my friends and my friends' friends knew, my dating life stalled. That is the bad thing about dating when you are over thirty-five; your pool of people becomes more like a kiddy pool. After dealing with that for a while, and panic had begun to set in, I decided I really needed to become proactive, really take charge. I was concerned that maybe those statistics that say you have more of a chance of getting hit by a meteorite than getting married after thirty-five were true after all. So I spent the next year or so asking everybody—and I do mean everybody—if they knew someone for me to date. I even had the ladies at the dry cleaner fix me up. They said he had nice suits.

Eventually I realized that I was reverting to my old self, back to the controlling woman who is not trusting God with the desire of her heart. And with similar, predictable results, I could feel the old, deceiver-fueled feelings bubbling up, anger and impatience that God had not provided what I wanted when I wanted it. But God is patient. And so good. His Spirit led me to pray for the strength to truly let go and to admit that God does not need my help to find me a husband. I prayed that prayer every morning.

The Encounter

You may be wondering if I ever crossed paths with Lew again in all that time after our relationship was finally over. I did, years later. I was with a girlfriend waiting for a table at a restaurant when I saw him come in. It felt exactly as you see it in the movies: a crowded, noisy restaurant, you see your former love across the room, and time stands still as your eyes meet, the room goes quiet, there's no one there but you and him. My heart really did skip a beat wondering what would happen when we spoke. What would I say? What would he say? But as he approached, a peace settled over me.

He said something lame like, "Hi, you guys here to get some lunch?"

Without skipping a beat I replied, "No, we heard they had air-conditioning and thought we'd come in and get cool."

He laughed that same familiar laugh I had once loved, we exchanged some other pleasantry, and he was gone. Casual banter between two people who would have been married now, probably with children, except for the fact that he left me at the altar, leaving me hurt and humiliated and broken for years. Casual banter as if nothing had ever happened. It was very weird.

My friend was the one who looked grief stricken, immediately wanting to know if I was okay, as if I might keel over right then and there. But you know what? I *was* okay. I assumed that was because God was holding me up so I wouldn't collapse from the weight of the encounter in the middle of the restaurant. I just knew that once I got in the car, I would break down. But I didn't. Not in the car, not when I got home, not the next day. Never. I was finally free!

A Happy Turn in the Road

After my year-long stint of missional dating and realizing that I needed to turn my search for a husband over to God and really mean it this time, my social life took a happy, contented turn. I think finally being able to do that proved more to me than to God. He knew all along that I could do it. I just needed to prove it to myself. And interestingly enough, once I seemed to be getting the hang of this trusting God thing, it spilled over into every other area of my life as well.

> "Kimberley, if you want a husband, pray for a husband. God will either give you a husband or change your heart and take away your desire."

What a joy it became to wake up every day and not feel the pull of my own self-will and desire for control, compelling me into situations at work, in relationships with my family and friends, or in anxiety about the future.

I won't say that I was anxious-free 100 percent of the time. There were moments I did worry that maybe I never would find anyone. I was going through a particularly lonely time when I asked a pastor friend of mine how it was that I should be praying. Was I supposed to tell God that I was okay with being single forever if that was his will for my life? If so, then I would probably never be able to do that, just being honest. The truth is, I wanted to get married. And I was concerned that my new-found walk with God had hit a real roadblock if I could not tell him that I could live with it if I never had a husband. What my pastor friend told me literally changed my entire outlook from that moment forward.

He said, "Kimberley, if you want a husband, pray for a husband. God will either give you a husband or change your heart and take away your desire."

Think about it. Either way, I win. And my reliance and dependence on God become complete.

A Husband of God's Choosing

Lauren wanted a husband. But at thirty-three, she was seriously begin-ning to wonder if it was ever going to happen. She had not dated that many men, but it seemed the few relationships she did have always ended the same way, with the men breaking it off with the line, "I just want us to be friends." That never feels good, I don't care how long you have been dating. One particular relationship ended, wouldn't you know, on Valentine's Day, when the man she had been seeing for about six months gave her a card that said, "It's great to have a friend like you." She can chuckle at that now, but at the time it was not so funny.

There would be yet another let's-just-be-friends relationship and several more years before the pivotal moment came in Lauren's life. She was on a Christian women's retreat when she told one of the leaders about her unfulfilled desire to have a husband and wondering, as I did, how she should be praying. The retreat leader told her not just to pray for a husband but to *boldly* pray for a husband. Lauren had never done that before. Sure, she had prayed for a husband, but always, she says, with an option clause: "God, please send me a husband *if it be your will because if it's not, I understand and will try to be happy living alone in my singleness.*" Lauren decided to give this new approach a shot.

Her mom happened to be along on this weekend retreat, so the two of them went to a beautiful nearby garden and prayed, boldly, specifically, for a husband of *God's choosing*, and this time with no option clause. They commissioned others to pray the same prayer.

Two days later Lauren met Ryan, who just happened to be the sound engineer for the retreat. A month later they met again at another retreat and struck up a friendship, her sharing her most recent break-up story and Ryan sharing his.

At first Lauren did not see what God had put before her. She saw Ryan simply as someone who could be a trusted friend. God clearly had other plans. That *friendship* blossomed quickly into romantic love, and ten months later they were married.

Lauren says that before Ryan she had always been the pursuer in her relationships, always giving more than she got in return. She knew Ryan was "the one" when she realized *he* was pursuing *her.* She finally realized that God wanted her to feel treasured by someone of *his* choosing. She just needed to be bold enough to ask.

The Preacher's Wife and the Pool Table

On the flip side is Mary. Her story is a perfect example of a woman for whom God did take away her desire for a husband. And in the process he proved what a great sense of humor he has.

Mary had been married to a minister, and together they lived on his family's big wheat farm in Kansas. But one New Year's Eve, Mary's husband decided that he did not want to be married anymore. So while she was away visiting a friend for the weekend, he packed his clothes and left, and when she returned Mary found a "Dear Jane" letter on the kitchen table. Mary never talked to him face-to-face again.

It was a cold way to end a marriage, for sure; so perhaps it is appropriate that he did it in the dead of winter. In Kansas that means it was extremely cold.

Mary was devastated, but she knew instinctively that her husband would not be coming back, so she packed her things and drove to Wichita where she worked. Now all she had to do was find a place to live.

After driving around for two days and spending the nights in an inexpensive motel, Mary went to work on Monday morning, leaving all her worldly possessions in her car. Can you even imagine how this woman felt? Her world had literally fallen apart, the man she had pledged her love and her life to had left her, and now she found herself alone (and cold) and at the mercy of some garage attendant to keep an eye on everything she owned.

The receptionist at the law firm where Mary worked was also single again and insisted that Mary come and stay with her as long as she needed. So Mary moved in with this kind woman.

There was just one tiny problem. The house only had furniture in one bedroom. But Mary discovered that there was a finished basement with a big closet, a fireplace, some furniture, and a pool table. No bed. Still, she was just thankful to have a roof over her head. So without skipping a beat, she took some sheets and blankets and pillows and made herself a bed . . . on top of the pool table.

In the following weeks, Mary actually found the basement to be quite cozy—a warm, quiet place to recoup and regroup. But in the middle of one night, she heard the call of nature. In the dark, she jumped down from her pool table/bed to head upstairs to the bathroom, but when she did, she landed in three inches of water. The basement was flooded. And the water was freezing.

> *How will I explain this to my family and friends? How about the preacher's wife got pneumonia because she landed in three inches of ice water when she fell off her pool table?* Not!

Mary says she was dancing around, trying to get out of the cold water when God reached down and tapped her on the funny bone. And rather than feel sorry for herself or cry or scream, she started to laugh. And laugh! And all she could think was: *How will I explain this to my family and friends? How about the preacher's wife got pneumonia because she landed in three inches of ice water when she fell off her pool table?* Not!

And at that moment, Mary says, the sun came up her in heart again. She was through crying over her loss, feeling sorry for herself, and blaming her husband for all her troubles. It was time to face the rest of her life and move on.

Looking back on all that had happened, Mary says she can now see that God had a plan for her all along. You see, Mary went on to have a very fulfilling career as a writer that also became her ministry. She truly believes that she never would have had time for these special opportunities if she had remained married because their life together had been all about *his* ministry.

Does she believe that God dissolved her marriage so that she could become a writer? No. But she does believe that in his foreknowledge, he knew it was going to happen and had Plan B in place and ready to go. He did exactly what he had promised—not to eliminate her problems but to walk through them with her and help her to come out on the other side alive and well.

Today, Mary says she is content being single. Her life is full with her writing, her church, her music, and her friends. God has so filled Mary with all of those things that there simply is no room for worry about not having a husband. And, no, she does not have a pool table.

The Dream

When we are so involved in controlling and running our lives, as I was, it is impossible to see God at work. For anything good that happens, we naturally give ourselves the credit, thinking we are responsible even though the Bible tells us that all good gifts come from him, more than we can even imagine or dream. But when we let God clearly and obviously have control of our lives, when good things happen, we *know* he is at work, and he gets the credit and the glory.

God so wants good things for us. I believe that if you want a mate, it is because God gave you that desire. He put it there. In my mind, the great God we worship is loving and kind and would not give us a desire for something he cannot give us. Yes, I know that is not always easy to believe. All these years after being left at the altar, God has not sent me this desire of my heart.

The wedding that I recount at the beginning of this chapter is a dream. It's how I envision my wedding day to be . . . someday—a day so different from the first in every way possible, but a day that reflects the person I have now become.

Yes, life is good. God has filled my life with a wonderful family and amazing friends, but for me, they cannot fill the space that only a spouse can fill. I believe that beautiful day will come because God has not taken away my desire for it. Still, I have to be honest and tell you there are many times I feel lonely, not for company, but for *him*, that person I believe is out there for me. Until then, I have peace and pray every day for that man, whoever he is, that God is preparing him for me and me for him.

What I have also come to realize is that "man's rejection, God's protection" does not just mean that God is protecting us from a bad relationship or a bad outcome. It also means he is protecting us *for* the one he has chosen. There have been several men who have come along that God has said no to, men who, to me, seemed like perfectly good prospects. But he said no, and I trust for reasons I may never know, that those men were not right for me. I want God to orchestrate the timing and the circumstances of my ultimate relationship. This time I'm doing things his way, and I have a sneaking suspicion that I'm going to be much happier with the results.

To put it in human terms, I love to make spaghetti for my niece and nephews. They love "Kiki's s'getti." It gives me great joy to make it for them because they love it so much, and it gives them so much pleasure.

When I know I'm going to make it for them for dinner, I'm excited all day. That is how I believe it is with God. He knows what he plans to do for us, whom he plans to give us, and he knows that it is going to bring us great joy and pleasure. I know how excited I get at making spaghetti

> This time I am doing things his way, and I have a sneaking suspicion that I am going to be much happier with the results.

for my sister's children, so I can only imagine how much greater is the Creator's excitement at giving us these desires of our hearts.

After all, we worship a God who excels at new beginnings. He gives us morning after night, spring after winter, *love after rejection*, and through the love of his Son, Jesus Christ, allows us to start over every day, forgiven of our failures and our fears. God does not keep an account of our failure to trust him before or after our rejections, and he does not want us to live in fear that we will never love again. Sometimes, though, God does allow us to sink so low that all we can see is up, and him. But that's not because he doesn't love us; it's because he *does*. He holds out his Fatherly hand, wanting us to take it. He wants to love us in our hurt, to heal us, and to ultimately draw us closer to him.

God has shown us, in the person of Jesus, the only One who will never reject us, never leave us, never disappoint or hurt us. As we move forward we must know that no person can ever be that fulfilling to us. Only Jesus. It is only when we accept that and believe it deep inside that we will finally be ready for God to bless us.

For many years I have carried in my Bible a letter that God might write to the single person. I have had it so long and read it so often that it is tattered around the edges, and the ink is getting faint. I would like to share part of it with you because it truly does feel as if God is speaking these words to me, lovingly and tenderly, knowing the loneliness I often have in my heart. The letter talks about how we all long to give ourselves completely to someone. But for those of us in faith, God will deny us that person until we can be content with being loved by him alone, exclusive of any other desire or longing. It tells us to stop planning and wishing but to wait. And it concludes by saying this:

> And then, when you are ready, I'll surprise you with a love far more wonderful than any you would ever dream. You see, until you are ready and until the one I have for you is ready, until you are both *satisfied with me* and the life I have prepared for you, you won't be able to experience the love that exemplifies your relationship with me, and this is the perfect love. And dear one, I want you to have this wonderful love. I want you to see in the flesh a picture of your everlasting union of beauty, perfection, and love that I offer you with myself.

Do you see? The man that God will send you will be the embodiment of *his* love for you.

I have this wonderful feeling that when God finally does send the one he has chosen for me, I'm going to shout out, "Thank you! Now I see why I had to wait so long!" I believe he is going to be far more wonderful than any man I could have imagined or would have chosen for myself. God's perfect gift. And then I will love again.

Not long ago, the Reverend Billy Graham's beloved wife, Ruth,

went to heaven. There was a
beautiful article in the paper
about her and their relationship.
Reverend Graham talked about
how grateful he was for the last
years of their lives together in
the mountains of North Carolina.

> I believe he is going
> to be God's perfect
> gift. And then I will
> love again.

"We've rekindled the romance of our youth," he said, "and my love
for her continued to grow deeper every day."[1]

Wow! What woman would not love to hear those words? A husband,
well into his eighties, remembering his wife of more than sixty years and
sharing how he loved her more every day. Those are not the words of a
man unsure of his feelings or not wholly committed to the relationship.
They are words of a man in love, pure and simple. And they are words
I pray someone will say about me one day. I have made up my mind, and
I pray that you will too, that nothing less will do.

At this moment, as you read this, you may not be in a place where
you can imagine falling or even *wanting* to fall in love again. You may
be so shattered by your rejection that that concept feels a lifetime
away. You may be so broken that you feel like you will never get put
back together again.

The Honeymoon

If you are in such pain, please know that there are people, like me, who
understand how your heart hurts. There is not a feeling of anger, self-
loathing, self-pity, or hopelessness that those of us in this club have

not experienced ourselves. But never forget the story of Leah, who may have lived in a world very far away from us now, but who experienced the exact same hurt of loving someone who did not love her back. Leah, like me, eventually found happiness and peace in knowing that her true worth came only from being loved by God.

Yes, it is excruciating and horrible to be rejected by someone you love. Believe me, I know. More importantly, never forget that your heavenly Father *knows too.* He is there in every single tear, in every single emotion. And through his love, the unmatched power of his Holy Spirit, and a little work on your part, you *will* laugh again, you *will* love again, and you *will* discover that you're pretty great after all.

When you fall in love with God, you can be assured of one very special thing: you will never be left at the altar. Instead, you will live with him happily ever after. And the honeymoon will never end.

Resource List

Am I Not Still God? by Kathy Troccoli, Thomas Nelson, Thomas Nelson, Inc., P.O. Box 141000, Nashville, Tennessee 37214, www.ThomasNelson.com.

Bad Girls of the Bible by Liz Curtis Higgs, WaterBrook Press, 12265 Oracle Boulevard, Suite 200, Colorado Springs, Colorado 80921, www.RandomHouse.com/Waterbrook.

Bumps Are What You Climb On, The by Warren W. Wiersbe, Revell Books, Grand Rapids, Michigan.

Getting Through the Tough Stuff by Charles R. Swindoll, Thomas Nelson, Thomas Nelson, Inc., P.O. Box 141000, Nashville, Tennessee 37214, www.ThomasNelson.com.

Grief Adjustment Guide by Charlotte Greeson, Mary Hollingsworth, and Mike Washburn, Questar Publishers, Sisters, Oregon. Out of print but usually available from www.amazon.com.

Hope in Pastoral Care and Counseling by Andrew D. Lester, Westminster John Knox Press, Louisville, Kentucky, www.wjkbooks.com.

Keeping a Princess Heart in a Not-So-Fairy-Tale World by Nicole Johnson, A Women of Faith® book, Thomas Nelson, Thomas Nelson, Inc., P. O. Box 141000, Nashville, Tennessee 37214, www.ThomasNelson.com.

Learning to Breathe Again: Choosing Life and Finding Hope After a Shattering Loss by Tammy Trent, Thomas Nelson, Thomas Nelson, Inc., P.O. Box 141000, Nashville, Tennessee 37214, www.ThomasNelson.com.

Start Where You Are: Catch a Fresh Vision for Your Life by Charles R. Swindoll, Thomas Nelson, Thomas Nelson, Inc., P.O. Box 141000, Nashville, Tennessee 37214, www.ThomasNelson.com.

Stronghold of God, The by Francis Frangipane, Charisma House, Lake Mary, Florida.

Acknowledgments

I saved writing these ackowledgments for last because I had a feeling they might be the most difficult. And when you are writing a book about getting left at the altar, that's saying a lot.

When I say "difficult," I mean that in a good way. I want to be certain my words convey my sincere, heartfelt thanks to these people who have meant so much to me and to getting this book to you, the reader.

As I reflect on this journey, I stand in awe once again of God and his amazing grace. The people he has used to get me to this place have each played a critical role. Some of them had major parts; two in particular provided just a sentence. All helped make this book possible. And I want them to know how deeply I love and appreciate them for being God's perfect gift.

First I want to thank all of the kind people, the strangers who knew me only from television, who sent cards and letters of encouragement after my very public rejection. Those notes gave me such hope and made me smile at a time when I did not feel like smiling. I'm so happy to have this opportunity to finally tell you how much they meant.

Thank you to my precious friends who encouraged me to finally tell my story and prayed for me throughout the process. Kathy Bremer, Nancy Tiller, Melissa Wright, and Joanne Joiner (Yours is one of the "sentences" I refer to. That is a lunch I will always treasure.) I am blessed to have all of you in my life.

A special thank-you to my friend Karin Smithson. Your counsel, advice, and wisdom—godly, worldly, and professionally—were invaluable. Besides my family you were my biggest cheerleader. Knowing you were there whenever I needed to bounce an idea or a theme off of you was like having a giant security blanket. I love being your friend.

To all of the professionals who helped me transform this from a skimpy manuscript to an actual *book,* thank you. Debbie Wickwire, thank you for recognizing that women need to hear this story of hope. I still can't believe I have in my corner someone in the publishing business as loved and respected as you. And thank you for sending me my brilliant editor and new friend, Mary Hollingsworth. Mary, I simply could not have done this without you.

To Blythe Daniel, my agent, thank you for everything. Your insight and knowledge taught me so much about being an author while your tender heart understood from the beginning what I wanted to accomplish with this book. From our very first phone call, I knew we would be more than agent and client. We are going to be girlfriends forever.

Thank you to all of the women who openly and lovingly shared your own personal stories of rejection and heartbreak. I am confident they will be inspiring to other women walking in your formerly painful shoes. As Jesus said, "This happened so that the work of God might be displayed in [your] life."

And to my family, Arch, Kathleen, and Mom: if only there were words to tell you how much I love you and how thankful I am to get to travel through life with you. You stood so firmly beside me, as you always do, during one of the worst things that could happen to a girl. You supported me, cried with me, fought for me, and prayed for me. You told me the truth when I needed to hear it and made me laugh when I needed that too. Kathleen, your own telling of *our* story provided such a rich part of this book. You managed to convey in such a real way the pain that we all felt. Thank you for your honesty, and I feel certain that God has now forgiven you. Kathleen, Arch, and Mom, all three of you fiercely love. How blessed I am to be the object of all that affection.

And finally, to my heavenly Father. I am blessed beyond measure to know you. You are my comforter, encourager, supporter, and biggest fan. I have loved every minute of writing this book alongside you. I pray it is what you intended and that, through these words that you have given me, other women will fall in love with you as I have. Thank you for loving me like no *body* ever will.

Notes

One: The End of Forever

1. Katharine Tynan Hinkson, "The Mist That's Over Ireland," *Irish Poems* (London: Sidgwick & Jackson Ltd., 1914).

Three: Suspended in Time

1. Charlotte Greeson, Mary Hollingsworth, Mike Washburn, *The Grief Adjustment Guide* (Sisters, OR: Questar Publishers, 1990), 68. Used by permission.

2. "Wild Flower," words by David Richardson. Copyright Edsel Music 1972, renewed 2000.

3. Greeson, op cit.

4. Andrew D. Lester, *Hope in Pastoral Care and Counseling* (Louisville, KY: Westminster John Knox Press, 1995).

5. Ibid.

Four: More Than Worthy

1. Erin Carlson, "The Bachelor Women: Are They Having Fun Yet?" Associated Press, April 17, 2007.

2. Sara Bunting, as quoted on www.TelevisionWithoutPity.com.

Five: The Perfect Target

1. Liz Curtis Higgs, *Bad Girls of the Bible* (Colorado Springs: WaterBrook Press, 1999).

Seven: Man's Rejection, God's Protection

1. Isabelle Holland, *The Long Search* (Greenwich, CT: Fawcett, 1992).

Eight: Left at the Altar Too

1. Sam Roberts, "51% of Women Are Now Living Without Spouse," *New York Times*, 16 January 2007, www.nytimes.com/2007/01/16/us/16census.html (accessed 5 August 2008).

2. Julie C. Wikel, Helen Gramotnev, and Christina Lee, "Never-Married Childless Women in Australia: Health and Social Circumstances in Older Age," *Social Science and Medicine*, vol. 62, issue 8, April 2006, 1991–2001.

Nine: The Hole in My Heart

1. Edward K. Kaplan, *Abraham Joshua Heschel: Prophetic Witness & Spiritual Radical: Abraham Joshua Heschel in America, 1940-1972* (New York: Yale University Press, 1998).

Ten: The Man's Perspective

1. Mignon McLaughlin, *The Neurotic's Notebook* (Indianapolis: Bobbs-Merrill, 1963).

2. Carol Gilligan, *In a Different Voice* (Cambridge, MA: Harvard University Press, 1993).

3. Deborah Tannen, *You Just Don't Understand* (New York: William Morrow, a division of HarperCollins, 1990). Reprinted by permission of HarperCollins Publishers.

4. Ibid.

5. Todd Sandel, Lifegate Counseling Center @ Peachtree, www.lifegatecenter.org.

Twelve: Laugh Again, Love Again

1. Gayle White, "Ruth Graham, Steadfast as Evangelist's Wife, Mother, Author," *Atlanta Journal-Constitution*, June 15, 2007, www.ajc.com/news/content/metro/obits/stories/2007/06/14/0614ruthgraham.html (accessed 9 June 2008).

Kimberley Kennedy is an Emmy Award-winning journalist and producer, writer, and host of a weekly newsmagazine show airing in Atlanta, Orlando, and Charlotte. As a former news anchor and reporter in Atlanta, she has covered stories ranging from fires and floods to the 1996 Summer Olympic Games, hosting a daily morning talk show.

Kimberley grew up in the tiny town of The Rock, Georgia. She graduated with a double major in English and political science from Agnes Scott College, where she was also associate editor of her weekly college newspaper. Kimberley is from a family of broadcasters: her sister, Kathleen, is a former anchor at CNN; and her brother, Arch, is a meteorologist in Nashville, Tennessee.

Kimberley serves as an elder at Peachtree Presbyterian Church in Atlanta and enjoys working for nonprofit organizations, public speaking, and being the world's greatest aunt to Reed, Joey, and Ryan. Kimberley lives in Atlanta, with not a single cat. You can visit her on her Web site: **www.kimberleykennedy.com**.